DEVELOPING ACTIVE READERS: IDEAS FOR PARENTS, TEACHERS, AND LIBRARIANS

Edited by
Dianne L. Monson
University of Washington
and
DayAnn K. McClenathan
State University of New York at Buffalo

D1561924

ira International Reading Association
800 Barksdale Road
Newark, Delaware

Copyright 1979 by the
International Reading Association, Inc.

Library of Congress Catalog in Publication Data
Main entry under title:

Developing active readers.

   Bibliography: p.
   1. Books and reading for children—Addresses, essays, lectures.
2. Libraries, Children's—Addresses, essays, lectures. I. Monson, Dianne L.
II. McClenathan, DayAnn K.
Z1037.A1D44   028.52   79-9058
ISBN 0-87207-727-6

Contents

Foreword

Literature has had an uneven journey across the frontiers of American reading instruction. Nila Banton Smith's monumental history (*American Reading Instruction*, IRA, 1965) documents that journey—from the didacticism of the nineteenth century to the classicism of the turn-of-the-century to the role of supplement to skills-laden reading lessons in more recent times. Today is different. There is evidence that literature for children and young people has arrived, to assume its place integral to the reading lesson.

The authors of this volume are aware of the newly evolved role of literature in the reading program. They are aware of the responsibilities it brings. They are concerned with its measurable effects on attitudes toward reading. They are concerned with selecting good literature from an offering so vast and varied that good taste may need to be re-defined. They are especially concerned with techniques to involve the reader—to foster response beyond the stock reply to the age-old question, "Did you like the story?" They are up-to-date, documenting the new importance of nonfiction and nonprint media to enhance the literary experience of children and young people.

Dianne Monson and DayAnn McClenathan are to be congratulated for assembling this volume. All the contributors deserve a careful, thoughtful reading. When the history of reading instruction is updated to include the contributions of our time, this set of readings will be a fine source of information. For the present, it is a valuable guide to theory and technique to advance the teaching of reading through literature. The volume is a welcome addition to the catalog of IRA offerings.

Sam Sebesta
University of Washington

Introduction

These last decades of the Twentieth Century are busy years for children as well as for adults. We are bombarded with print and nonprint media, tantalized by the world that may lie beyond our known solar system, and faced with numerous problems on our own small planet. Children growing up now must cope with an overwhelming number of verbal and nonverbal channels, some trying to entertain, others giving information. Out of these experiences, children fashion a sense of the world and begin to build the understandings which they will use in later years to deal with the exigencies of life.

Good books should be an important part of growing up because they deal with many of the universal questions people have struggled with over the centuries. Good literature gives children a chance to experience situations in which story characters must weigh the worthwhile against the trivial, the good against the evil, the value of true friends against the attraction of easy popularity. Independent reading provides something that television cannot—the chance to stop and think about a story, to consider how it relates to a reader's life, and to think about ways the book may help with understanding life.

Books can also serve as socializers in the sense that they provide natural situations for discussion between parents and children, teachers and children, and among peers. The notion of informal discussion is important. So many things have cut into the time parents and children have together that many children have almost no opportunity to carry on a dialogue with an adult. Yet language skill, beginning with oral language and discussion, is an important background for learning to read. Parents who share books with children can, at the same time, give children something to talk with them about.

The focus on hearing or reading books (sometimes followed by discussion or another kind of activity) is suggested with the hope that it will produce readers who respond actively to literature—who enjoy it, value it, and will make reading a lifetime habit. With that in mind, this pamphlet has been organized in two parts: the first section gives ideas for book selection and introducing children to libraries; the second section recommends some means of helping children interact more completely with books. We hope these ideas will lead to many valuable home and school reading experiences.

DLM
DKM

Part One
The Right Book for Each Child: Book Selection and Library Use

The keys to producing dedicated readers lie in acquainting children with the range of books available and helping them to recognize and expand their interests. Beyond that, they must learn how to locate the books they will find most satisfying.

The Dulin article provides two useful instruments—one designed to look at attitude toward reading and the other a means of looking at reading interests. Students can learn about themselves by examining their attitudes toward reading. Students and teachers can use the interest scales to lighten the job of finding a "good book to read."

The articles by Carlson and McClenathan examine some of the reading options for contemporary children as well as some of the problems in dealing with controversial books. Guidelines are given for using books which may be considered controversial.

Zaidi emphasizes the importance of introducing young readers to nonfiction so that they develop the skills and experience necessary for comprehending the range of materials that are not fiction. The last two articles in Part One, by Miller and Alongi, are concerned with ways parents, teachers, and librarians can acquaint children with the many resources available in the library.

Assessing Reading Interests of Elementary and Middle School Students

Ken L. Dulin
University of Wisconsin at Madison

The measurement and evaluation of various aspects of students' affective orientation toward reading and reading materials have long been topics of concern to teachers. This presentation focuses on three new measurement tools: 1) an *attitude* inventory designed for assessing elementary and middle school students' general feelings toward reading; 2) an *interest* inventory designed to tap these students' preferences within and among various reading topics, reading genre, and print forms; and c) a *motivational* survey designed to plumb the relative motivational appeals various teacher procedures and classroom practices hold for these students. Materials included are copies of the three instruments, scoring and interpretation procedures for each, and initial validation statistics for all three.

The Wisconsin Reading Attitude Inventory, Form II

This questionnaire (really a *battery*) has four distinct parts, each of which can be used separately or in combination with any or all of the other parts.

Part I is the Dulin-Chester Scale, the second version of a project Bob Chester (now of the University of British

Columbia) and I began about two years ago. Since that time, this scale has been administered to several thousand children, has proven to be quite reliable, and has been published in *Tests and Measurements in Child Development: Handbook II,* Orval G. Johnson, Editor, Jossey-Bass Publishers; and in *Teaching Children to Read,* Richard J. Smith and Dale D. Johnson, Addison-Wesley Publishing.

The Dulin-Chester Scale is scored fairly simply. All the *odd numbered items* (1, 3, 5, 7, and so on) are scored 1, 2, 3, 4, or 5 from the left hand box to the right hand box; and all the *even numbered items* (2, 4, 6, 8, and so on) are scored 5, 4, 3, 2, or 1 from left to right. When summed, then, the total scores possible from this section can run from a low of 20 to a high of 200, with the 45 to 65 range of scores seen, as a result of our past testing, as "average."

Part II of the total inventory is the Estes Scale, developed by Tom Estes of the University of Virginia and first published in the *Journal of Reading,* November 1971. It's scored by awarding individual points of 5, 4, 3, 2, and 1 to As, Bs, Cs, Ds, and Es for all of the *positive* items (2, 5, 7, 10, 14, 15. 18, and 19) and awarding 1, 2, 3, 4, and 5 to As, Bs, Cs, Ds, and Es for all of the *negative* items (1, 3, 4, 6, 8, 9, 11, 12, 13, 16, 17, and 20). Here, too, the summed scores can run from a low of 20 to a high of 100, with the 65 to 90 range seen as average. The Estes Scale, updated and revised, is available with scoring keys and manual, from the Virginia Research Association, Box 5501, Charlottesville, Virginia 22902.

Part III was simply a little experiment Bob and I were interested in, since it used a ratio kind of measurement (i.e., the dividing up of the parts of a constant sum to show relative attitudes), and so we include it. Surprisingly, it turned out to be a quite good measurement device. When we added together the number of points the subjects gave to the first two categories, "Reading Books" and "Reading Magazines and Newspapers," we found that sum correlated highly with all of our other measures.

Part IV consists simply of some self-rating scales. We used them (plus many other things) as criterion measures during our field testing.

FORM II

THE WISCONSIN READING ATTITUDE INVENTORY

Ken Dulin and Bob Chester
The University of Wisconsin at Madison

NAME _____ DATE _____

SCHOOL _____ TEACHER _____

GRADE IN SCHOOL _____ SEX _____

(circle one)

DIRECTIONS

The test you're about to take is called an "attitude inventory." Instead of measuring what you KNOW, it is designed to measure how you FEEL about something. This particular attitude inventory deals with books and reading.

I. The first part of the inventory consists of a series of choices to be made between different leisure-time activities, some dealing with reading and others not. You're to indicate your choices by marking a series of scales, and it works like this.

At each of the two ends of each scale there'll be an activity, something you could do in your spare time if you wanted to. If you'd *much* rather do one of the activities than the other, mark the box *nearest to* that activity, like this:

read a book | X | | | | watch TV

or

read a book | | | | X | watch TV

Or, if you'd *sort of* rather do one or the other, mark the box *second* from that activity, like this

read a book | | X | | | watch TV

or

read a book | | | X | | watch TV

Or finally, if the two activities are *absolutely equal* in your mind, mark the middle box, like this

read a book | | | X | | watch TV

Now go on to the real choices.

4   Dulin

WHICH WOULD YOU RATHER DO?

THIS...	OR	THIS...
1. listen to the radio		read a book
2. read a book		clean up around the house
3. play a musical instrument		read a book
4. read a book		shine your shoes
5. write a letter		read a book
6. read a book		watch television
7. play with a pet		read a book
8. read a book		take a nap
9. do some work around the house		read a book
10. read a book		read a magazine
11. draw or paint a picture		read a book
12. read a book		fix something to eat
13. call a friend on the phone		read a book
14. read a book		play a solitary game
15. read a newspaper		read a book
16. read a book		look at pictures
17. do a cross-word puzzle		read a book
18. read a book		work on a craft or hobby project
19. work on a school assignment		read a book
20. read a book		listen to records

II. Now, to take the next part of the inventory, you're to *grade* twenty statements in terms of how you feel about them. If you STRONGLY AGREE with a statement, give it an A; if you TEND TO AGREE with it, give it a B; if you feel FAIRLY NEUTRAL about it, give it a C; if you TEND TO DISAGREE with it, give it a D; and if you STRONGLY DISAGREE with it, give it an E. Be sure to read each statement carefully before you circle a grade for it, and be sure to grade *every* statement.

1. Reading is for learning but not for enjoyment.　　　　　　A　B　C　D　E

2. Money spent on books is well-spent.　　A　B　C　D　E

3. There is nothing to be gained from reading books.　　　　　A　B　C　D　E

4. Books are a bore.　　　　A　B　C　D　E

5. Reading is a good way to spend spare time.　　　　　　A　B　C　D　E

6. Sharing books in class is a waste of time.　　　　　　　　A　B　C　D　E

7. Reading turns me on.　　A　B　C　D　E

8. Reading is only for grade grubbers.　A　B　C　D　E

9. Books aren't usually good enough to finish.　　　　　　　A　B　C　D　E

10. Reading is rewarding to me.　　A　B　C　D　E

11. Reading becomes boring after about an hour.　　　　　　　A　B　C　D　E

12. Most books are too long and dull.　A　B　C　D　E

13. Free reading doesn't teach anything.　　　　　　　　　A　B　C　D　E

Dulin

14. There should be more time for free reading during the school day.   A   B   C   D   E

15. There are many books which I hope to read.   A   B   C   D   E

16. Books should not be read except for class requirements.   A   B   C   D   E

17. Reading is something I can do without.   A   B   C   D   E

18. A certain amount of summer vacation should be set aside for reading.   A   B   C   D   E

19. Books make good presents.   A   B   C   D   E

20. Reading is dull.   A   B   C   D   E

III. This third part of the inventory calls for a bit of math ability. Your job this time is to *divide up 100 points* among the following ten things in terms of *how desirable* you feel they are as leisure activities. Remember, the total should come out to 100.

Activities	Points
Reading books	
Reading magazines and newspapers	
Watching television	
Playing musical instruments	
Doing craft and hobby work	
Listening to the radio	
Writing letters	
Listening to records	
Painting or drawing pictures	
Sleeping or napping	
Total	100

IV. And finally, to tell us a few things about *yourself*, please respond to the following three scales by circling the answer to each which *best describes you.*

1. Compared to other people your own age, about *how well* do you think that you read?

1	2	3	4	5
a good deal better than most	somewhat better than most	about as well as most	somewhat less well than most	a good deal less well than most

2. Compared to other people your own age, about how much do you feel you *like to read?*

1	2	3	4	5
a good deal more than most	somewhat more than most	about as much as most	somewhat less than most	a good deal less than most

3. And finally, compared to other people your own age, about how *much* reading do you feel you do?

1	2	3	4	5
a good deal more than most	somewhat more than most	about the amount as most	somewhat less than most	a good deal less than most

Thanks for your participation. Now please turn this in to your teacher.

The Dulin-Chester Reading Interests Questionnaire

This instrument combines two things: The survey of reading interests by topics, genre, and print forms; and the motivational survey regarding teacher procedures and class-room practices.

The project was developed for the reading people of the Oconomowoc, Wisconsin, Public Schools. It has also been used in many other places, and has been slightly adapted for other applications. It has turned out to be highly reliable and quite useful.

The scoring is quite straightforward, simply the conversion of the A-B-C-D-E grades to numbers (5, 4, 3, 2, and 1) in parts I through IV and the retaining of the raw scores in parts V through VII. When we conceptualized the parts as we were developing them, we looked upon Part I as dealing with Reward Systems, Part II as dealing with Teacher Motivational Devices, Part III as dealing with Follow Up Activities after a lesson, and Part IV as Enrichment Activities after a lesson. Part V is Topics about which to Read, Part VI is Reading Genre, and Part VII is Reading Print Forms.

As far as "norms" are concerned, this concept doesn't really mean much related to an interest inventory; more important is the fact that the instrument appears to be quite reliable (gives consistent information).

READING INTERESTS QUESTIONNAIRE
Ken Dulin and Bob Chester
The University of Wisconsin at Madison

Name _____ Date _____

School _____ Grade _____ Teacher _____

Some of us like to read a lot and others don't, but almost all of us read at least sometimes for one reason or another. That's what this questionnaire is about: *why* people read.

I. Sometimes for example, people read because their teachers or parents *reward* them for reading.

Here are ten possible rewards a person could get for reading, some of them pretty good rewards and some others not so good. To show how *you* feel about each of them, *grade* each reward, A or B or C or D or E. Here's what each grade means:

A = I feel this would be a *very good* reward for reading.

B = I feel this would be a *fairly good* reward for reading.

C = I feel this would be only an *average* reward for reading.

D = I feel this would be a *fairly poor* reward for reading.

E = I feel this would be a *very poor* reward for reading.

For each reward, circle the grade you're giving it.

1. getting a grade for how much reading you do   A   B   C   D   E

2. getting extra credit for how much reading you do   A   B   C   D   E

3. getting your name on a bulletin board for how much reading you do   A   B   C   D   E

4. getting stars on a chart for how much reading you do   A   B   C   D   E

5. getting money for how much reading you do   A   B   C   D   E

6. getting prizes for how much reading you do   A   B   C   D   E

7. getting free time in school as a reward for extra reading you've done   A   B   C   D   E

8. getting a certificate to take home for extra reading you've done   A   B   C   D   E

9. getting to go to other classes to tell about books you've read   A   B   C   D   E

10. getting excused from other class work as a reward for extra reading you've done   A   B   C   D   E

II. Sometimes things *teachers* do encourage us to read. Please grade the following ten things to show how much you think they'd encourage *you* to read. Here's what the grades mean this time.

A = I feel this would *certainly* encourage me to read.

B = I feel this would *probably* encourage me to read more.

C = I feel this *might* encourage me to read more.

D = I'm pretty *sure* this *wouldn't* encourage me to read.

E = I'm *quite sure* this *wouldn't* encourage me to read more.

Again, circle the grade you're giving the activity.

1. having the teacher read a book to
   the class at a chapter a day

   A   B   C   D   E

2. having the teacher read to the class
   the first few pages of books that you
   can then check out if you want to

   A   B   C   D   E

3. having the teacher act out parts of a
   story or book before you start to
   read it

   A   B   C   D   E

4. having the teacher take your class
   to the school library now and then

   A   B   C   D   E

5. having the teacher tell you about
   the lives of authors of books you
   can read

   A   B   C   D   E

6. having the teacher tell about the
   places where stories in books take
   place

   A   B   C   D   E

7. having the teacher tell about books
   he or she has read

   A   B   C   D   E

8. having the teacher explain some of
   the hard words in a book or story
   before you read it

   A   B   C   D   E

9. having the teacher give you some
   oral questions about a story in a
   book before you start reading it

   A   B   C   D   E

10. having the teacher give you some
    written questions to answer *while*
    you're reading a story or book

    A   B   C   D   E

III. Now, here are some things you might do *after* reading a book or story in class. Grade them by these grades.

A = I'd *like* to do this.

B = I'd *sort of* like to do this.

C = I'm *not sure* if I'd like to do this.

D = I *don't think* I'd like to do this.

E = I'm *sure* I wouldn't like to do this.

1. take a written test on how well you understood a story you've read   A   B   C   D   E

2. take a written test on how much you can *remember* about a story you've read   A   B   C   D   E

3. take an oral test on a story or book you've read   A   B   C   D   E

4. use some of the new words in a story or book you've read for word-study   A   B   C   D   E

5. write a book report about a book you've read   A   B   C   D   E

6. give an *oral* report on a book you've read   A   B   C   D   E

7. write your own ending to a story or book you've read   A   B   C   D   E

8. do a crossword puzzle with some of the new words in a story or book you've read   A   B   C   D   E

9. match some of the new words in a story or book you've read with their definitions   A   B   C   D   E

10. take a spelling test on some of the new words in a book or story you've read   A   B   C   D   E

IV. And finally, here are some *extra* things you could do after reading a story or book. Grade them with *these* grades.

A = I'd *really like* to do this.

B = I'd *sort of* like to do this.

C = I *might or might not* like to do this.

D = I'm *fairly sure* I wouldn't like to do this.

E = I'm *quite sure* I wouldn't like to do this.

1. make a play out of a story or book you've read   A   B   C   D   E

Dulin

2. make a picture to go with a story or
   book you've read   A   B   C   D   E

3. have a discussion in class about a
   story or book you've read   A   B   C   D   E

4. write a story of your own about
   people you've met in a story or book   A   B   C   D   E

5. go to a movie or play made from a
   story or book you've read   A   B   C   D   E

6. meet the author of a story or book
   you've read   A   B   C   D   E

7. listen to a record of an author reading his or her own story   A   B   C   D   E

8. look at pictures of the people you've
   read about in stories or books   A   B   C   D   E

9. look at pictures of the places you've
   read about in stories or books   A   B   C   D   E

10. have the school librarian visit class
    and tell about books you can read   A   B   C   D   E

V. That's all the grading for you to do. This time you're to
number certain kinds of reading to show how you feel. Give your
favorite thing to read about number 1, your next favorite number 2, and
so on, down to number 10. Here are your choices. Be sure to give *every
type of reading* some number.

TYPE OF READING	NUMBER
about sports and athletics	
about hobbies and crafts	
about travel and faraway places	
about animals and pets	
about adventure and romance	
about careers and occupations	
about religion and religious people	
about science and inventions	
about science fiction and tales of the supernatural	
about detective stories and mysteries	

VI. These next two parts of the questionnaire will call for a bit of Arithmetic ability. This time you're to *divide up 100 points* (think of dividing a dollar into cents) among five kinds of reading to show how much you like each of them. Each kind can get anywhere from 0 points to the whole 100, but remember that *the overall total must equal 100.* Here they are.

KINDS OF READING	POINTS
full length books about imaginary people	
nonfiction stories and books about real-life people	
short stories about imaginary people and events	
plays	
poetry	
TOTAL	100

VII. And finally, for the last part of the questionnaire, *divide up 100* points to show how much you like different *types* of reading material. Any one type can get from 0 to 100 points, but you should try to give at least *some* points to each.

TYPES OF READING MATERIAL	POINTS
magazines	
newspapers	
comic books	
hardbound books	
paperback books	
TOTAL	100

That completes the whole questionnaire. Thanks for finishing it all. Later on your teacher may share with you how most of your class felt about all these things. Now please turn in your questionnaire to your teacher.

Using These Instruments

The best uses of the reading attitude measures would probably be as measurements before and after some sort of experimental treatment (say, a USSR program) or simply as overall measures of fall to spring changes in your students. Also, you might want to use the basic scores yielded by the various scales as guides to grouping practices, to individual counseling, or to other curricular decisions.

As for the Reading Interests and Teaching Practices instrument, we found at Oconomowoc that many interesting relationships were uncovered when we compared the interests and opinions of high, average, and low ability groups of students and high, average, and low attitude groups of students.

This instrument has been published in the same handbook mentioned above for the Dulin-Chester Scale and served as the basis for several research papers presented at the Great Lakes Regional IRA Conference in Milwaukee.

Book Selection for Children of a Modern World

Ruth Kearney Carlson
Hayward State College

Last week I walked down the halls of an Albany Elementary School and noticed a little blond fifth grade child stumbling along the corridor as he read an article, "How to Rewrite Your Way into a PhD." I didn't stop him as I didn't want to disturb his engrossed perusal of this adult type article. But I shall be forever curious about this boy's selection of reading matter.

Several years ago I was a consultant to a school library in the small community of Rodeo. One of my professional duties involved assistance in the selecting of books. I was discussing book selection with a group of about thirty children who were suggesting choices of books they would like to have purchased. One sixth grade child said, "I would like to have more books about China." She had read every book about China which she could find at the local branch library and Contra Costa Library. I thought I could expand her interest horizons through changing the geographical locale such as using books about Tibet, Vietnam, Korea, Cambodia, and Thailand. After introducing other countries, I again asked her to state her choice and she said, "I want some more books about China." This child had already selected her area of interest.

A third example concerns a group of boys in Hayward, California, who belonged to a Bug Club sponsored by Gladys Conklin, the children's librarian. The club was so successful that boys devoured every avaiable book on bugs and insects.

One boy went to the adult section and selected a mature, encyclopedic style of book about insects. The adult librarian felt its reading level was much too difficult, but the child was intellectually prepared to use that book. He did not know some of the scientific words in the text, but he was able to do many things with charts, graphs, and pictures.

These three examples, the boy's reading about rewriting skills, the girl's asking for a book about China, and the boy's seeking out an adult scientific book on insects, illustrate one problem of book selection—the selection of the right book to meet the needs of *an individual child* at the right time.

Books for Schools and Libraries

A second type of book selection concerns the choice of books for a school or a public library. Librarians and book selectors have used certain basic criteria of selectivity. One helpful aid to these persons is *A Critical Handbook of Children's Literature* (19). Lukens outlines such items as character, plot, setting, theme, point of view, style, and tone.

In her article, "If That Don't Do No Good, That Won't Do No Harm: The Uses and Dangers of Mediocrity in Children's Reading," Egoff (9) cautions us to be wary of mediocre books. Egoff states that all persons concerned with children's reading—writers, publishers, editors, teachers, booksellers, librarians, parents—must decide whether to use careful planning on book selection or the laissez faire principle where books of any kind might be acceptable. Egoff made a rough survey of the quality of books listed in *Children's Books in Print* which consists of approximately 41,000 titles. She states, "of this number two and one half percent are excellent, 35 percent are perceptibly sludge and dross, and the rest are in between, that is, mediocre."

One basic problem in book selection is its relationship to book banning or censorship. If provocative or controversial books are selected, some of the reading public are apt to protest about a portion or the entire book. Marjorie Fiske made a study of California librarians and found a majority of them were guilty of self-censorship. They refused to buy or, having bought, hid away those books which they feared might arouse public outcry (*9*). This comes under the category of social responsibility.

Egoff feels that the role of literature is to help develop the individual. This takes a good book. In her words, "A poor book takes a child and puts him back a step or two, a mediocre book takes a child and leaves him where he is. A good book promotes an awareness of the possibilities of life, the universality of life, the awakening of response."

Mediocrity in books provides certain outlooks which are commonplace. We underestimate children. Slow learners and poor readers are just as interested in ideas as are quick readers. Mediocre books rarely get challenged by adults. They have commonplace, dully written pages and seldom take strong stands for certain causes. Mediocre books build laziness in young readers. As long ago as 1924, Alice Jordan stated "Mediocrity in books for children is more universal and more baffling to combat than sensationalism" (*9*). Mediocre books usually present a narrow view of life and do not translate well, so they cannot affect other world cultures.

Many novels for adolescents and young adults are quite mediocre. In 1955, Richard Alm analyzed a group of junior novels. He called many of them "sugar puff" stories, lacking in insight and writing ability. He said the stories were superficial, often distorted, sometimes completely false representations of adolescence. He also castigated them for their representations of stock characters, easy solutions to problems, model heroes, saccharine sentiment, oversimplification, single motivation, and inconsistencies in characterization, as well as indications that nothing is impossible and maturity is attained without development. He recognized the better qualities of *Seventeenth Summer* (Daly) and others by Cavanna, Felsen, and Stolz. He categorized four books as outstanding: *The Yearling* (Rawlings), *Johnny Tremain* (Forbes), *Goodbye My Lady* (Street), and *Swiftwater* by Annexter (*15*).

McQuown (*20*) criticizes teenage books for girls which conform to a pattern:

> A teenage romance is a book written to fairly rigid specifications between the ages of twelve and eighteen. The heroine should be a person of upper middle class and she must have a problem to solve. The problem must be solved in approximately 200 attractively bound pages

in reasonably good English, with virtue triumphant. One of the serious failings of writing to such a pattern is that the characters are cardboard and the plots contrived. Stereotyped characters and unconvincing plots may emerge as a result of unskillful writing, but I suspect that, in the case of the teenage novel they arise from a strict and narrow form.

Igo (*16*) has pointed out that most of the world's greatest literature is controversial. He felt that contact with such books may do less harm than contact with second rate books, for second rate books come from second rate minds, and it is better to leave people to make their own spontaneous approach to life than to clutter their thinking with cliche responses. On the other hand, contact with a variety of original, first rate minds might make a bastion against pressures toward conformity which in large part are overwhelming motion pictures, radio, television, and the press.

One way for book selectors to determine books which seem relevant is to make a survey of books children or young adults are actually reading. Campbell, Davis, and Quinn (*6*) made a survey of young adult reading interests in the Los Angeles Public Library and Alm (*2*) made reading profiles from nine Hawaii High Schools. Investigators of reading interests of Los Angeles teenagers using the public libraries sent out questionnaires. Out of 2,009 responses received on books actually read, five titles were top favorites:

1. *My Darling, My Hamburger* (Paul Zindel)
2. *Mr. and Mrs. BoJo Jones* (Ann Head)
3. *Go Ask Alice* (Anon)
4. *Catcher in the Rye* (J.D. Salinger)
5. *Bless the Beasts and Children* (Glendon Swarthout)

The survey of Hawaiian high schools indicated different choices:

1. *The Godfather* (1969)
2. *Love Story* (1970)
3. *Mr. and Mrs. BoJo Jones* (1967)
4. *The Catcher in the Rye* (1951)
5. *Lord of the Flies* (1955)
6. *Lord of the Rings* (1954, 1955, 1956)

7. *To Kill a Mockingbird* (1960)
8. *Black Like Me* (1960)
9. *Flowers for Algernon* (1966)
10. *The Outsiders* (1967)
11. *Gone With the Wind* (1936)
12. *Catch-22* (1955)

If books were selected based upon the interests of readers, much more banning of books would probably ensue. It looks as if there is a real generation gap between selections made by librarians and school boards and those made by children and adolescent readers. A frightening article, "Banning Books: An Ancient Sport Makes a Rowdy Comeback Among School Boards," appeared in the May 1973 issue of the *American School Board Journal* (3). An excerpt from this article states:

> In Ridgefield, Connecticut, a middle-aged widowed school teacher found her dog, a pet poodle, hanging by its choke collar in a tree in her yard. In this same town automobile tires have been slashed, a school board meeting was interrupted because of a bomb threat, 360 teachers in the school district threatened to strike, the superintendent was fired after six years on the job, and armed guards have manned the doors of the public board of education meetings. Why this? The school board and twenty thousand people of this no longer sleepy New England town are involved in a controversial current event book banning.

During Selection of current literature for a high school level English class in the Rochester Public Schools, much controversy was centered on Kurt Vonnegut's *Slaughterhouse Five* (*10*).

Criteria for Selection

Simpson (*25*) cited four criteria for the selection of a book, a film or a record which were suggested by John Rowe Townsend: 1) popularity or potential popularity, 2) relevance, 3) literary merit, and 4) suitability or appropriateness to the supposed user. Critics have described Junior Novels as pablum or fluff. Now such books as *Go Ask Alice, Run Shelly Run,* and *The Chocolate War* take a reverse trend. Critics who formerly asked for an honest story about serious teenage problems have begun protesting again. In the words of Simpson (*25*), one hears "Language like that in a book for young people? Are rape, abortion, homosexuality, unwed mothers, suicide, drugs, unsympathetic portrayal of parents, and violence appropriate subjects for junior novels? Are young people ready for such explicit realism? Would you want your daughter to read one?" Simpson has paraphrased Ivan Southall in the words, "If we feed children and young adults a steady diet of pap, of the false, the trivial, the phoney, we will produce adults who will continue to believe lies and cheap sentimentalities because they do not know truth." An article by the ALAYASD Medial Selection and Promotion Committee surveys media under "Loving Choices." This reviews media concerned with teenage premarital pregnancies, new life styles of marriage, venereal disease, homosexuality, and other social problems. A rash of stories for young people was called "The Grouping Group." Some of these were *Dinky Hocker Shoots Smack* (Harper & Row), *I Will Go Barefoot All Summer for You* by Katie Letcher (Lippincott), and Isabelle Holland's *The Man without a Face* (Lippincott) (*1*).

In addition to traditional criteria for book selection, current book selectors are confronted with the new realism in children's books. With the onslaught of modern sociological changes in our society, some feel that childhood innocence is gone. Three sources on controversial issues in children's literature are Carlson's "Controversial Issues in Children's Literature" (*7*), Rudman's *Children's Literature, An Issues Approach* (*22*), and *Issues in Children's Book Selection* (*17*). Some of the issues discussed at great length in the Rudman book are siblings, divorce, death and old age, war, sex, Blacks, Native Americans, and females.

In addition to these issues, violence and aggression are becoming major issues in current, modern, realistic fiction as well as in television programs. A frightening discussion of violence of the worst kind appears in an English publication, *Children's Literature in Education 8*. In this journal, Salter (*24*) has written an article entitled "The Hard Core of Children's Literature." He discusses the violence in *Skinhead, Suedehead*, and *Boot Boys* by Richard Allen. In eighteen months, more than 200,000 copies of *Skinhead* had been sold, and by October 1978 it had been reprinted seven times. Another 250,000 copies of *Suedehead* and *Boot Boys* had been sold. *Suedehead* was reprinted four times within four months after its publication in October 1971. According to Salter, "All these books are written in the same formula, incidents of sex and violence, usually linked, follow rapidly upon one another within a plot that is sufficiently vague and unrestricted to allow frequent explosions of violence." Violence is the principal selling point of *Chopper* as seen in this excerpt:

> Chopper moved into position. The skinhead was still bent double. Bringing up his knee, Chopper felt with satisfaction the scrunch of broken bone as the kid's nose made contact. The kid went down, while blows from boots rained upon his body. He lay groaning, spitting out gouts of deep red blood and pieces of broken teeth.

This description seems gory but it is subdued when compared with the scalping of a fourteen year old Pakistani boy in *Mama*, a follow up to *Chopper*. This is not only violent but it has a racist quality. Repetitively in *Skinhead* and *Suedehead*, "the crunch of breaking bone was a glorious sound." Again, "His next blow broke the man's jaw, the crunch bringing a measure of satisfaction." "Cracking bone increased Joe's desire to inflict pain" or "Chopper brought up his knee under the kid's face and felt the personal satisfaction of hearing the crunch of broken bone from his nose." In the Allen books, violence is seen as a source of pleasure. Rarely do characters show hesitation in inflicting pain as cited by Salter (*24:47*):

> Joe Hawkins had a "feeling" for violence. Regardless of what do-gooders and sociologists claimed, some people had an instinctive bent for creating havoc and resorting to jungle savagery. Joe was one of them.

Richard Allen's books also have many racial stereotypes. Jews have hooked noses and names like "Hymie Goldschmidt." An American hippie thinks about "Uncle Sam" and the "hoosegow" and an Irish landlady, Mrs. Malloy, talks about "the Auld Sod."

Choosing Modern Literature

Selecting ethnic literature which is honest and authentic and yet devoid of racial stereotypes is another basic problem in choosing modern literature for the child of the seventies and eighties. Much ethnic literature is controversial. In an article entitled "A Study of Conflicting Values," Broderick (4) speaks of *provocative* books. She discusses *Two Blocks Apart* by C.L. Mayerson (Holt, 1965). This is the story of the affluent Peter Quinn, who is upper middle class Irish Catholic, and Juan, a lower class Puerto Rican Negro, raised a Catholic but no longer finding a meaning in religion.

Broderick points out that a great book might not provoke the reader. It can meet the fundamentals of esthetic criticism and be worthy, but it may not question the world of established values. Some books such as *Durango Street* (Frank Bonham) and *Ring the Judas Bell* (J. Forman) may be provocative without being great. Broderick states that James Baldwin "reads books to identify himself as a member of the human race, with knowledge that he is not alone in being different in suffering" (4). This feeling for humanity is reinforced in *A Time to Be Human* by John Howard Griffin (12).

Numerous sources are available on the selecting of good ethnic literature. Such books and media should be honest, authentic, lack negative stereotypes, and present a true picture of the racial identity of the principal characters. They should not present characters as inferior because they represent a different culture or way of life. They should present true images of Blacks, Chicanos, Jews, Indians, Chinese, or any group of people offering a way of life different from the White Anglo-Saxon Protestant. *Now Upon A Time: A Contemporary View of Children's Literature* (23), in a section called "The American Mosaic," presents a discussion of the Black experience in Children's Literature as well as chapters on Native Americans, Jewish Americans, and other selected minority groups.

An Eric report summarizes the work of the NCTE Task Force on Racism and Bias in the Teaching of English. In its "Criteria for Teaching Materials in Reading and Literature," five deficiencies were seen: 1) inadequate representation of nonwhite minorities in general anthologies; 2) representation of minority groups which is demeaning, insensitive, or unflattering to the culture; 3) inclusion of only popular and proven works by a limited number of "acceptable" writers; 4) biased commentaries which gloss over or ignore the oppression suffered by nonwhite minority persons; and 5) commentaries in anthologies which depict inaccurately the influence of nonwhite minority persons on literary, cultural, and historical developments in America (8).

Numerous professional articles have been written concerning the distortions of Indian images in literature for children and adolescents. In "That's One Good Indian: Unacceptable Images in Children's Novels," Herbst(13) states that 1) the Indian in the standard novel is often portrayed as inferior to the white culture so his life may be improved if he abandons his Indian way of life; 2) he is a savage and worth only annihilation; and 3) quaint and superficial treatment is given without any depth or warmth.

Byler (5) states that there are probably too many books about Indians:

> There are too many books featuring painted, whooping befeathered Indians closing in on the many forts, maliciously attacking "peaceful" settlers or leering menacingly from the background; too many books in which white benevolence is the only thing that saves the day for the incompetent childlike Indian; too many stories setting forth what is "best" for American Indians.

Byler also feels that too many stories for very young children are about little boys running around in feathers and headbands, wearing fringed buckskin clothing and moccasins, and carrying little bows and arrows. The author speaks fervently, as she is of an Eastern band of Cherokee Indians.

Mickenock's article (21) "The Plight of the Native American," discusses negative images. One fact which is frequently ignored is that as early as 1637, the Puritans began the practice of scalping by offering rewards for scalps with the ears of their enemies attached. The author of this article is a member of the Ojibway Nation.

Many librarians and curriculum specialists wonder about requests for the banning of *Little Black Sambo* which, on the surface, seems like a harmless little book. Yuill (28) has written an enlightening article entitled "Little Black Sambo: The Continuing Controversy." Knowledgeable specialists in children's literature have spoken out against objectionable themes, stereotyped illustrations, degrading names, and exaggerated dialect. Stereotypes and caricatures appear in most earlier versions of *Little Black Sambo*. Characters had big lips, large white eyes, and a curly head of hair (like a mop). Mumbo was shown as a fat, barefoot Aunt Jemima, and Sambo was sometimes depicted as a silhouette in a forest, or as a little nude boy running in and out among the trees. Yet thousands of copies of *Little Black Sambo* are being sold annually in spite of negative stereotypes that appear on many pages of this little book.

In addition to selecting books devoid of excessive violence and literature which presents authentic images of minority cultures, a major problem is the one of language used by authors to present a character or an aspect of the plot. Language which is offensive to some persons seems appropriate to others as a means of character development and portrayal. Some critics feel that language which is nonoffensive and vapid destroys the authenticity of a character; others feel that words which are offensive to some ears may lead to book banning and censorship. Some persons' ears are not attuned to the cursing which appears in many modern children's books. Much discussion has ensued concerning Johanna Reiss' *The Upstairs Room*, a Newbery Honor Book. Mary F. Poole, a librarian in Durham, North Carolina, states that this book had more than fifty irreverant expletives and one four letter word. In an article entitled "Expletives Deleted: More Reactions to Censorship of Cursing in Children's Books," several different opinions appear about so-called "dirty language" (*11*).

Some critics scurry through pages of children's books searching for expletives and curse words. Charlotte Church of the Williamstown Public School Library in Massachusetts did not detect a flaw of language in *The Upstairs Room* because the book had reality and authenticity, but she resented the use of the word "bastard" in Thomas Rockwell's *How to Eat Fried Worms* (Watts, 1973). She states, "I thoroughly enjoyed the delightful audacity of this book until page 92, where one child calls another 'a bastard.' I have marked the word 'bum' in its place in my copies" (*11*). This reminds us of librarians who painted diapers on the nude boy in the book *In the Night Kitchen* by Sendak.

Another librarian, Linda R. Silver, perhaps with tongue in cheek, suggests the following use of symbols for reviews in the *School Library Journal* (*11*):

* = 1-5 swear words
** = 5-10 swear words
! = sex
*! = swearing and sex

She also suggests an alternative in which publishers might delete objectionable words or passages and leave blank spaces. Then librarians or readers could put in their own words such as, "My Gosh," exclaimed Peter, as the Gestapo shot his parents.

The Child as a Literary Critic

Numerous books and articles have been written on literary criticism but few of them have considered the possibilities of the child as a literary critic. Glenna Davis Sloan (*26*) has written an illuminating book entitled *The Child as Critic: Teaching Literature in the Elementary School*. The author feels that children can make valid judgments concerning good books if they are taught some of the structural principles of literature. For example, children might learn four basic plots: romance, tragedy, satire and irony, and comedy. Children can also be trained to consider literary questions such as Did the story end as you expected it to? Did the author prepare you for the ending? How? Suppose you had a different ending for the story. How would you have the rest of the story changed for the new ending?

Kingston (*18*) teaches both children and adults to consider the tragic content in children's literature through her book, *The Tragic Mode in Children's Literature*. The author suggests five tragic moments: rejection, entrapment, sensitivity, war, and loss. Perhaps "entrapment" needs some explanation. In the words of Kingston, "With their backs against the wall, these tragic heroes find their way through their own enlarged and enduring capacities." For example, *The Road to Agra* by Aimee Sommerfelt is a story of a lowly brother and sister who seek help against the impending blindness of the girl. They have one difficulty after another, but they endure and Maya is healed and her brother comes to a greater sense of self-realization. *Where the Lilies Bloom* by Vera and Bill Cleaver presents a group of children who feel entrapped by villagers who might send them to an orphan's home because the children have no parents. But Mary Call, through one desperate measure after another, saves the family from starvation and separation. She grows stronger in the process.

Tway (27) has written a brief article entitled "Literary Criticism for Children" in which she suggests numerous questions which reflect upon the structural phrases of good books: "What was the truth as the author saw it? Did the author tell who, what, when, and where and convince you? Did the author *build* his story well? Did the author appeal to more than one sense? Did the author choose a point of view that helped tell the story in the best possible way? Did the author present enough detail to give you a feeling of reality?"

This selection of specific detail is a major help in getting the reader *involved* with the characters in a book. One child read a book in which the author said, "Wine and cakes were served." The reader tossed the book aside in disgust with the words, "I don't want general words, I want to know what kind of wine and what kind of cakes."

Such detail is available in the series by Laura Ingalls Wilder, including *By the Shores of Silver Lake, Little House in the Big Woods, Little House on the Prairie, On the Banks of Plum Creek,* and *Farmer Boy.* When Wilder describes a storm, you can hear the wind howl through the chinks of a cabin and feel the cold wetness of fluffy snowflakes drifting down on your head or the tip of your nose.

W.H. Hudson was a compulsive writer who felt that a book for children should represent the best efforts of the author and that many young readers could detect the technical beauty within a literary work of art. He sensed the mystique of nature and used close observational skills. In *A Little Boy Lost,* Martin is lost and sits down to rest as he is hot and tired. Here is an excerpt quoted by Higgins (14) in his book, *Beyond Words*:

> ... he shed one little tear. There was no mistake about the tear; he felt it running like a small spider down his cheek, and finally he saw it fall. It fell on a blade of yellow grass and ran down the blade, then stopped so

as to gather itself into a little round drop before touching the ground. Just then, out of the roots of the grass beneath it, crept a tiny, dusty black beetle and began drinking the drop, waving its little horns up and down like donkey ears, apparently very much pleased at its good fortune in finding water and having a good drink in a dry, thirsty place. Probably it took the tear for a drop of rain just fallen out of the sky.

"You are a funny thing!" exclaimed Martin, feeling now less like crying than laughing.

The wee beetle, satisfied and refreshed, climbed up the grass blade, and when it reached the top lifted its dusty black wing cases just enough to throw out a pair of fine gauzy wings that had been folded up beneath them and flew away.

Such writing causes a reader to burrow into the pages of a book, to look at little things in the natural world with a greater sense of wonder, and to appreciate the beauty of life. We should depend more upon helping young readers to become critics of the structural beauty of books and we should select more children to be members of our book selection committees.

References

1. ALAYASD Media Selection and Promotion Committee. "Loving Choices," *Top of the News*, January 1974, 191-204.
2. Alm, Julie N. "Young Adult Favorites: Reading Profiles from Nine Hawaii High Schools," *Top of the News*, June 1974, 403-409.
3. "Banning Books: An Ancient Sport Makes a Rowdy Comeback among School Boards," *American School Board Journal*, May 1973, 25.
4. Broderick, Dorothy M. "A Study of Conflicting Values," *School Library Journal*, May 1966, 17, 23.
5. Byler, Mary Gloyne. "The Image of American Indians Projected by Non-Indian Writers," *School Library Journal*, February 1974, 36.
6. Campbell, Patty, Pat Davis, and Jerri Quinn. "We Got There...It Was Worth the Trip! A Survey of Young Adult Reading Interests in the Los Angeles Public Library," *Top of the News*, June 1974, 394-402.
7. Carlson, Ruth K. "Controversial Issues in Children's Literature," *Enrichment Ideas*, Second Edition. Dubuque, Iowa: Wm. C. Brown, 1976.
8. Dieterich, Daniel J. "Books that Lie and Lullabye," *Elementary English*, November 1972, 1003.
9. Egoff, Sheila. "If that Don't Do No Good, that Won't Do No Harm: The Uses and Dangers of Mediocrity in Children's Reading," *Issues in Children's Book Selection: A School Library Journal/Library Journal Anthology*. New York: R.R. Bowker, 1973, 4, 5, 7.
10. Escott, Richard H. "Everybody's Talking at Me," *Top of the News*, April 1975, 296-330.
11. "Expletive Deleted: More Reactions to Censorship of Cursing in Children's Books," *School Library Journal*, September 1974, 49.
12. Griffin, John Howard. *A Time to Be Human*. New York: Macmillan, 1977.
13. Herbst, Laura. "That's One Good Indian: Unacceptable Images in Children's Novels," *Top of the News*. January 1975, 192-198.

14. Higgins, James E. *Beyond Words: Mystical Fancy in Children's Literature.* New York: Teachers College Press, 1970, 12.
15. Hutchinson, Margaret. "Fifty Years of Young Adult Reading 1921-1971," *Top of the News*, November 1973, 33.
16. Igo, John. "Books for the New Breed," *Library Journal*, April 15, 1967, 1704-1705.
17. *Issues in Children's Book Selections: A School Library Journal/Library Journal Anthology.* New York: R.R. Bowker, 1973.
18. Kingston, Carol T. *The Tragic Mode in Children's Literature.* New York: Teachers College Press, 1974, 59-60.
19. Lukens, Rebecca L. *A Critical Handbook of Children's Literature.* Glenview, Illinois: Scott, Foresman, 1976.
20. MacQuown, Vivian J. "The Teenage Novel: A Critique," *Library Journal*, April 15, 1964, 1832.
21. Micknock, Rey. "The Plight of the Native American," *School Library Journal*, September 1971.
22. Rudman, Marsha Kabakow. *Children's Literature: An Issues Approach.* Lexington, Massachusetts: D.C. Heath, 1976.
23. Sadker, Myra Pollack, and David Miller Sadker. *Now Upon a Time: A Contemporary View of Children's Literature.* New York: Harper and Row, 1977.
24. Salter, Don. "The Hard Core of Children's Fiction," *Children's Literature in Education 8.* London: Ward Lock Educational, 1972, 39-55.
25. Simpson, Elaine. "Reason, Not Emotion," *Top of the News*, April 1975, 301-303.
26. Sloan, Glenna Davis. *The Child as Critic: Teaching Literature in the Elementary School.* New York: Teachers College Press, 1975, 78.
27. Tway, Eileen. "Literary Criticism for Children," *Elementary English*, January 1967, 62-63.
28. Yuill, Phyllis. "Little Black Sambo: The Continuing Controversy," *School Library Journal*, March 1976, 71-75.

Realism in Books for Young People: Some Thoughts on Management of Controversy

DayAnn K. McClenathan
State University of New York at Buffalo

Several years ago when I was participating in IRA's Rocky Mountain Regional Conference in Denver, I noticed that Lloyd Alexander was giving an address with a catchy title, something like, "The Gentle Reader or Keeping Sex, Violence, and Death in Children's Books Where They Belong." Whether we think they should be there is not the issue, really; that's where you'll find them. To acknowledge is not necessarily to endorse; but not to acknowledge suggests unforgivable ignorance.

Emergence of Controversial Issues

Controversy in children's books is not a new development. About ten years ago when I first started teaching literature for children we worried about content, but the dilemma involved qualitative criteria for the most part. Should we permit, encourage, or more or less ignore it when kids come to school with a new comic book in the hip pocket every other day? Should children be permitted to stay "in a reading rut" so to speak, with Nancy Drew or the Hardy Boys? These were real concerns and maybe still are or should be, but such questions are easily eclipsed when one of Nancy Drew's literary descendants has gotten into drugs or is trying to decide whether to have an abortion.

Since such heavy philosophical decisions are inevitably going to dominate this analysis, it may not be entirely inappropriate to inject a single humorous note in an attempt to keep a balanced perspective. It seems that comic books, bugbear nonpareil to so many English and reading teachers over the years, are undergoing changes of a somewhat different nature. My aunt, an elderly and venerable author, was recently contacted by someone connected with the Diocese of Cincinnati about doing a series of comic books on the Lives of the Saints! Ah, the irony of it all. Has the day perhaps arrived when we will be saying to the kids, "What are you reading that twenty-one chapter hardback realistic fiction for? That's junk. Try a good, wholesome, uplifting comic book instead."

Anyway, the emergence of controversial issues in children's books—the newer ones, the braver ones—is itself a "hot issue" these days. Authors and publishers are meeting head-on some of the concerns which engage the attention of young people in the real world. The proof that they are scoring in the interest category is that the books are being read, discussed, recommended and, in many cases, reread by the audiences for which they are intended. What more can we hope for? My somewhat irreverent two word answer to that is—a lot.

Before investigating the questions associated with separating wheat from chaff and considering which books, volatile though they may be, are worth using with young people (even though some school and community management strategies may have to be employed), a look at some of the books and the issues they raise would seem appropriate. Some of us, busy beyond belief with the countless demands imposed by our professional roles, don't even have the time or opportunity to know what the provocative issues are until a particular book launches some kind of an explosion at a PTA meeting and we are caught wondering what all the furor is about.

Change in Children's Books

Perhaps a useful way to go about examining change in children's books is to identify departures from traditional themes.

Children's books involving interrelationships with members of the same family have always been popular. But a "family" story of the seventies may include divorced or divorcing parents, retarded siblings, eviction, a senile grandparent in the home, someone who is involved in drug rehabilitation, a father who is unemployed, or an uncle who has recently been released from prison.

Stories about friendship may now involve specific heterosexual encounters, homosexuality, communal living, experimenting with drugs, or coping with the need for an abortion. Interestingly, one of the most poignant developments in several recent books, set both within and without the family circle, involves attention to the details of poverty and the sometimes brutal behavior engendered by impoverished circumstances.

New books offering realism in terms of shift away from stereotypes of females and blacks appear every year, and this momentum is now being observed in increasing numbers of books about Native Americans, Chicanos, and Puerto Ricans.

Are there distinctions to be made here to help us decide what is both appropriate and artistic? What books are unquestionably worthwhile because they help us perceive human options and better understand the human condition? Unfortunately, arguments about literary quality sometimes disappear in the face of topical taboos, and the result can be that a poor book is given undue attention simply because it deals with a timely issue of great personal interest to young people.

Why bother with volatile topics in fiction, anyway? Isn't it safer to avoid the onset of a problem by leaving such books off the shelves in schools and simply ignoring them when they show up around the building in the hands of the students? Besides encouraging overt censorship, wholesale avoidance is inappropriate for a number of reasons, some of which follow:

1. A book about a relevant sociological or psychological problem can give young people valuable opportunities to stretch and grow in the thinking process, to extend experience, and to distill meaning.
2. Problems in books can provide children who need them with opportunities for identification. For chil-

dren to whom the element of identification does not apply, there is the equally valuable opportunity to sympathize with those who are less fortunate.

3. Children cannot be expected to develop values in a vacuum. Problems in books invite decisions, elicit opinions, afford opportunities to take positions on issues, and encourage the formulation of judgments.

4. Contact with provocative books may just be unavoidable at times. If boys and girls are passing around a current favorite and it is very obviously engaging much of their time and attention, you will almost have to get into the act for reasons having to do with classroom management.

If you are planning a somewhat structured literature experience with a book which may entail reading aloud, sharing views, or writing critiques, a rule of thumb might be not to go out of your way to select a book you very definitely dislike. Your nonobjectivity will probably be apparent to the children and some of them may automatically pick up your attitude. It is always wise to remember that taste and appreciation in books are highly personal. Guiding a discussion is one thing, but hoping that students will emerge from a contact with literature reflecting your views defeats a valuable opportunity to nurture their own critical thinking. Furthermore, you would probably not want to get deeply involved in a provocative topic about which you were insufficiently informed (such as certain aspects of drug use) because this would doubtless necessitate having a resource person on hand to help you whenever a discussion got underway.

Guidelines for Selecting Books

When you are planning to use books in your classroom (for whatever reason, be it a lesson in literature or simply a talk session about what everybody seems to be reading on his own anyway), you might find the following guidelines helpful:

1. *Know exactly what the problem is and consequently what might be considered controversial.* This means you have to really *read* the book. You can't rely on the

opinion of someone else or even on a good review. It's necessary that you, as a member of school and community, be able to appraise specific content in light of the mores of that particular milieu. What might offend in one community would go unnoticed or unchallenged in another.

2. *Ascertain the author's point of view and weigh the power of positive influence against exposure to a negatively perceived theme.* If an author writes about the drug culture, for example, but events in the story clearly point up harmful effects of drug use, then reluctance to use the book may result in a missed opportunity for healthy shaping of attitudes.

3. *Apply literary criteria to the selection of library books in such a way that vulnerability to the arguments of would-be censors is at least partially reduced by the obvious overall quality of book choices.* Occasionally, inferior quality books are selected because they deal with topics having a high interest quotient for middle grade or older children. This sometimes happens with books involving experimentations with sex. The information in such a book may be harmless (or even useful) but the book may fall short of accepted literary criteria. If the book is then targeted because it offends community groups, it will be difficult to defend, and having it in your school collection will suggest that considerations other than literary quality determine choices. In addition to generally accepted literary criteria, you will want to examine books which attempt to counter stereotypes for what can be thought of as the overcorrection syndrome. Sometimes, in a passion to change images, authors will work too hard on the issue itself with the result that plot and characterization suffer. (Sadker and Sadker in *Now Upon A Time*, Harper & Row, 1977, offer useful criteria for selecting library books.)

4. *Know and be able to explain your purpose in using a particular book.* Have answers ready to the following questions:
   a. Will the topic be understood by the group with which I intend to use the book?

b. What are some of the merits of this particular book which have influenced me to use it, rather than another book of comparable literary, sociological, or psychological importance?
c. Is the book an acceptable model in terms of writing style and use of language?
d. Are my objectives in using this book educationally defensible (e.g., presentation and/or clarification of information, extension of experiences, refinement of attitudes, promotion of the reading habit)?

5. *In order to clarify and maintain your own sincere objectivity, review and be prepared to discuss both sides of the censorship question.*

From the Primary Reading Program to the Library

Louise J. Zaidi
Sacramento, California, Public Schools

Too often the primary reading program is limited to the use of one or two basic reading series. The key word here is *limited*, for it is desirable that the classroom teacher use one or more basic reading series or programs. In these, the vocabulary, word attack skills, comprehension skills, and concept development are sequentially structured. Even if every teacher were capable of developing a reading program, time does not permit such activity. Besides, this is somewhat akin to each person's rediscovering the wheel.

Sound pedagogy dictates that learning should (and does) proceed from the known to the unknown and that school experiences should be predicated upon the concept of taking learners from where they are to as far as they are capable of going. It is this concept upon which the principle of individualizing instruction is based. A prerequisite to an effective program of individualized instruction is a large variety of books and materials of varying topics, levels of difficulty, and tasks to be performed. An obvious source for such a variety of materials and media is the library. Thus, basal readers or other programs should be the beginning of the primary reading program. The limits should be determined only by the limits of materials and media that are available in the library and the teacher's resourcefulness in using them. But how can we take the primary reading program, which begins with basal readers or other materials in the classroom, to the many varied books and materials in the library?

Introducing Children to Nonfiction

Much of the material that children are exposed to in early instruction is narrative. Children learn to recognize such stories as typical of material they can read in books from the classroom and school libraries. They learn how to read narrative, how to comprehend it, how to answer the kinds of questions teachers are likely to ask about such stories. Indeed, children learn to read and comprehend narrative passages quite well, especially those most similar to the syntax of the children's oral language (3: 112-113). Surely the time spent in practicing the reading of narrative day after day has some influence on that performance.

If we look at children's reading interests, it is evident that they like to read about topics presented in nonfiction library material (1, 2). However, the children in one study of second grade reading ability did a poor job of comprehending expository, or nonfiction, writing even when it was written so that the syntax was closely related to the students' own oral language (3: 109). The lack of experience with nonfiction in basal reader instruction may have strongly influenced that rather surprising outcome.

It has been pointed out that basal readers need not—and should not—be the only material that primary age children read. The library is a rich source of nonfiction which can help to provide the exposure and practice needed to develop facility in reading and understanding such material. Children are interested in animals as pets. Many have cats, dogs, hamsters, gerbils, and rabbits as pets at home or in the classroom.

The number of library books giving information about animals is increasing each year. Library books on other science related topics are also likely to be intrinsically interesting to children. Tresselt's *The Beaver Pond*, Selsam's *Let's Get Turtles*, and Phleger's *The Whales Go By* are examples of books written at a level young readers can handle. Bernice Freschet has several books appropriate for young readers: *The Flight of the Snow Goose* and *The Web in the*

Grass. For more confident primary readers, add McClung's *How Animals Hide* and Carla Stevens' *The Birth of Sunset's Kittens*. *The Emperor Penguins* by Kazue Mizumura is a "Let's Read and Find Out Science Book" for primary children. *Let's Find Out about Birds* by Martha and Charles Shapp, *The Air We Breathe* by Enid Bloome, and *We Like Bugs* by Gladys Conklin are a few examples of the many interesting books on science topics written for young readers. All of these books give information in a straightforward fashion and deal with questions children often raise.

"How to" books are also interesting to children as they begin to realize that they can, indeed, *use* what they read. Hudlow's *Eric Plants a Garden* can be read by a confident second grade reader as can Lopshire's *It's Magic?*, Moore's *The Seabury Cookbook for Boys and Girls*, Sokol's *The Lucky Sew-It-Yourself Book*, and Unkelbach's *You're a Good Dog, Joe: Knowing and Training Your Puppy*.

There are fewer books for this age group that deal with topics related to social studies, but even here books are available for young students who are gaining in ability to read independently. Patricia Lauber's *Too Much Garbage* identifies an ecological problem that children are aware of, as does Peter Parnall's *The Mountain* which shows how pollution can ruin the beauty of the wilderness. Robert Quackenbush's *Take Me Out to the Airfield*, about the Wright brothers and their airplane, gives an idea of the historical importance of the airplane as a means of transportation. One class of second graders was very interested in the description of how to build an airplane. "The True Books" (*The True Book of Transportation*) and the "I Want to Be" books (*I Want to Be a Pilot*) by Children's Press are books on social studies topics written at a primary level which children may be interested in reading. A book which may interest young boys is *The Road Builders* by James Kelly and William Park.

These and many other books are available in school libraries. They will give children a chance to expand their interests at the same time that they gain practice in reading for information. Librarians and teachers working together to get children into readable and interesting nonfiction books can add an important dimension to the reading program.

Techniques for Encouraging Children to Read

To expand reading horizons beyond the limits of basal readers, we need to incorporate in the primary reading program activities both in and out of the library. This will also expand children's perceptions of reading to include the concept of communication between writer and reader. Perhaps we can also develop a habit of reading for enjoyment as well as for information and reading as a subject in school.

To begin with, children should be taken to the library to explore. Let them see books on many subjects to arouse their curiosity and to get them to ask about things. If a child asks the teacher to read a book that arouses interest, the teacher should do so. If the book is easy enough, after the teacher has read it, the child may want to check the book out and read it. Even if the student only "reads" by reciting it from memory, it is a good beginning to reading and building the child's self-concept concerning ability to read. It also helps build the concept that reading is the acquisition of meaning and that the library is a good place to go if one wants to find out about things. In other words, the library should be thought of as more than just a place to go to check out a book to take home.

Some reading class sessions can be held in the library rather than in the classroom. Perhaps no other technique will do as much as this will to reinforce the concept that reading is more than a subject in school and that library material is an integral part of the reading program.

After use of the library has become an accepted part of the reading program by both teachers and children, thought and planning should be given to selecting materials and activities from the library to coordinate with, and supplement, stories read in basal readers. Supplemental books on the same topic or theme can be used. Many of the basal reader series include stories that are either taken from or adapted from children's books. At the time of reading these stories the original books can be brought into the classroom.

Some stories in basal readers use classic themes in children's literature with which most children are familiar. Two examples of this are: "And He Did" in *Around the City*, Bank Street Readers primer, which uses the theme of "The Little Red Hen"; and "Flossie Flamingo" by Harriette H. Miller in *How It Is Nowadays*, Level 8 reader of Ginn's Reading 360 Series, which uses the theme of "Chicken Little." When these stories are read, a discussion of the theme should follow. Some children may be interested in reading the classic.

Supplementary library books about the topic read can be brought into the classroom. For example, if the story read in the basal reader is about dogs, books about dogs can be obtained from the library. Or if the story concerns a common or current human or environmental problem, some children may be interested in reading library books on the same topic. In each case the teacher may bring the supplemental books into the classroom, or the teacher and/or librarian can help children find books in the library on the same topic.

Children can participate in storytelling, story hours, short skits, and simple puppet plays that use hand puppets, stick puppets, and bag puppets which they can easily make. The skits and puppet shows can be extemporaneous to check comprehension after the story is read. Summer school programs can include story hours involving the activities just described.

Successful reading experiences develop positive self-concepts and positive attitudes about reading, and they also provide reinforcement of skills. The following four factors are important objectives in a successful primary reading program: 1) developing a positive self-concept, 2) developing positive attitudes about reading, 3) providing successful reading experiences, and 4) providing a variety of reading activities.

Syntactic, semantic, and concept repetition occurs in basal reader stories, and these stories can be effectively read in the classroom using choral reading techniques. Many library materials are available for supplementary activities in the library. Such materials lend themselves to reading in a variety of ways. Sometimes children will enjoy reading the stories silently. They can also be read orally in a number of ways. Children can read them in unison as in choral reading. A technique that is effective with beginning readers calls for the teacher to read the story while children read the repeated parts in unison. Some books that can be effectively used this way are *Brown Bear, Brown Bear, What Do You See?* by Bill Martin, Jr. and *Captain Murphy's Tugboats* by William Hall. Or children may be grouped and when the teacher reads the story, the groups can take turns in reading the repeated parts. These are only a few suggestions for reading this type of material. Teachers and children may think of other ways.

The primary reading program does not have to be limited to one or two basal readers to be read only in the classroom. By going beyond the classroom to the library, reading horizons and children's perceptions of reading are broadened. Children can begin to develop reading habits and the habits of using the library.

Children's Books

Black, Irma Simonton, et al. *Around the City.* Bank Street Readers Primer. New York: Macmillan, 1965.

Bloome, Enid. *The Air We Breathe.* Garden City, New York: Doubleday, 1971.

Clymer, Theodore, et al. *How It Is Nowadays.* Level 8 Reading 360 series. Lexington, Massachusetts: Ginn, 1973.

Conklin, Gladys. *We Like Bugs.* Illustrated by Artur Marokvia. Holiday House, 1962.

Freschet, Bernice. *The Flight of the Snow Goose.* Illustrated by Jo Polseno. Crown, 1970.

Freschet, Bernice. *The Web in the Grass.* Illustrated by Roger Duvoisin. Scribner's, 1972.

Greene, Carla. *I Want to be a Pilot.* Children's Press, 1960.

Hall, William. *Captain Murphy's Tugboats.* Illustrated by William Krasnoborski. Holt, Rinehart and Winston, 1967.

Hudlow, Jean. *Eric Plants a Garden.* Whitman, 1971.

Kelly, James, and William R. Park. *The Road Builders.* Drawings by Joel Snyder. Addisonian Press Book, 1973.

Lauber, Patricia. *Too Much Garbage.* Garrard, 1974.

Lopshire, Robert. *It's Magic?* Macmillan, 1969.

Martin, Bill, Jr. *Brown Bear, Brown Bear, What Do You See?* Holt, Rinehart and Winston, 1963.

McClung, Robert. *How Animals Hide.* National Geographic, 1973.

Mizamura, Kazue. *The Emperor Penguins.* New York: Thomas Y. Crowell, 1969.

Moore, Eva. *The Seabury Cookbook for Boys and Girls.* Illustrated by Talivaldis Stubis. Seabury, 1971.

Parnall, Peter. *The Mountain.* Doubleday, 1971.

Phleger, Fred. *The Whales Go By.* Illustrated by Paul Galdone. Random, 1959.

Posell, Elsa. *The True Book of Transportation.* Children's Press, 1960.

Quackenbush, Robert. *Take Me Out to the Airfield.*

Selsam. *Let's Get Turtles.* Illustrated by Arnold Lobel. Harper, 1965.

Shapp, Martha and Charles. *Let's Find Out About Birds.* New York: Franklin Watts, 1967.

Sokol, Camille. *The Lucky Sew-It-Yourself Book.* Illustrated by Bill Sokol. Four Winds, 1966.

Tresselt, Alvin. *The Beaver Pond.* Illustrated by Roger Duvoisin. Lothrop, 1970.
Unkelbach, Kurt. *You're A Good Dog Joe: Knowing and Training Your Puppy.* Illustrated by Paul Frame. Prentice, 1971.

References
1. Butler, James Orval. "Expressed Reading Preferences of Children Enrolled in Grade Two in Selected Schools of Colorado," unpublished doctoral dissertation, University of Oklahoma, 1964.
2. Peterson, Gordon Charles. "A Study of Library Books Selected by Second Grade Boys and Girls in the Iowa City, Iowa Schools," unpublished doctoral dissertation, University of Iowa, 1971.
3. Zaidi, Louise J. "Differences in Sentence Structure in Narrative, Exposition, and Children's Oral Language and Their Effects on Comprehension at the Second Grade Level," unpublished doctoral dissertation, University of Washington, 1974.

The Primary Child in the Library

Margaret J. Miller
Longview, Washington, Public Schools

On their own in a world of exploding knowledge? The library is the place for children to start applying language skills on the road to independent lifelong learning.

Acquiring survival skills in the world of literature and information necessitates a base of positive attitudes. If the child feels that

> listening is enjoyable;
> reading is enjoyable;
> acquisition of knowledge is desirable;
> a library user should ask for help when needed;
> materials should be returned on time;
> materials, equipment, and facilities must be kept
>   in order and used correctly; and
> the library is an interesting place,

then the teachers and library personnel have been setting the stage for the pupil's continued growth as an active learner who knows that

> use of materials is profitable in gaining knowledge;
> acquisition of retrieval skills is useful;
> library workers are important;
> voluntary service is worthwhile; and
> everybody should become a regular, independent
>   library user.

How? Not without teacher-librarian cooperation in developing lesson sequences that teach and reinforce in both the classroom and the library. Frequent incidental teaching and learning as opportunity arises can pave the way for the more formal skills and understandings.

Library Media Skills and Understandings

Kindergarten
- Awareness of the library
- Listening to a story
- Participating in literature through puppetry and drama
- Learning library citizenship
- Learning about the parts of a book, selecting a book
- Circulation of books, book care, and the Dewey Decimal System of Classification

Grade 1
- Awareness of author and illustrator
- Recognizing alphabetical order
- Learning to locate books
- Learning about the types of materials available (records, study prints, magazines, globes, etc.)
- Learning about audiovisual usage
- Using recreational materials such as games, flannelboard, autoharp, tonebells, puzzles, Viewmaster
- Practicing library citizenship
- Using numerical order (Dewey numbers) to locate books
- Carrying out research and reporting using reference books
- Beginning volunteer service as a library aide

Grade 2
- Differentiating fiction and nonfiction
- Developing awareness of Caldecott Award books
- Using the card catalog, subject cards
- Locating books by using library signs, numerical order, Dewey numbers, and coding
- Learning about maps and newspapers as new types of materials

- Increasing audiovisual usage
- Practicing research and reporting, using such techniques as skimming, writing short answers, citing sources, distinguishing dictionary from encyclopedia use

Grade 3
- Becoming familiar with physical location of materials
- Learning about the atlas
- Locating materials by using bibliography and mediography
- Learning to use reference books
- Learning more about the parts of books (glossary, bibliography, chapter, index, title page, endpaper)
- Learning about publishing and publishing terms
- Learning how libraries acquire books (from suggestion slip to evaluation, purchase orders, jobbers, shipment)
- Learning about author cards and title cards in the Card Catalogue
- Learning about the public library
- Adding to ability to use the Dewey Decimal System
- Continuing to work on research and reporting

Primary research need not be an awesome task for the child if it is started early, tied to expressed or potential interest, kept within the capabilities of the student, and carried out sequentially. Young researchers, greeted at the gates of knowledge by enthusiastic library personnel and intelligently guided by cooperative professional preplanning, bubble with the thrill of finding out.

Research and reporting activities handled in bite-size pieces are the natural complement to the child's innate desire to learn. Some primary teachers keep a research roster so that different pairs of children have an investigative experience as questions come up in the classroom during the year. Others survey the availability of materials with the librarian and set up success laden questions beforehand.

On their own in an overwhelming multimedia world? Provide individualized activities tailored to the library to be used. Library personnel along with teachers can develop a master file of task cards, numbered to indicate approximate grade level difficulty. These can be utilized to prescribe an independent or lightly supervised activity for an individual student according to ability. Volunteer parents and tutors can assist children. Although the possibilities are numerous, a few ideas are illustrated on the chart shown on pages 48-50.

Kindergarten
1. Find books about animals that live underwater. Make an underwater picture.
2. Given a collection of books, put them into piles of tall and short books, thick and thin books.
3. Tell the story of a wordless book onto a tape. Use the subject heading STORIES WITHOUT WORDS to find a book.
4. Use a *beginner's dictionary*. Draw pictures of three words that begin with *b*.
5. The name of a book is called a *title*. The *title* is on a library book in at least four places. Find the *title* in three places.

First Grade
1. Look at these two *magazines*: *Wee Wisdom, Ranger Rick*. Tell which one you like best and why. Check one out.
2. Look at the *newspaper*. Find pictures that show these feelings: happy, sad, angry. Cut out the pictures. Paste them on a paper. Write the feeling words under the pictures.
3. Look at a book of paintings. Find three paintings you like. Write the *page numbers* of the pictures. What is the *title* of the book?
4. Look at the zoo animal *study prints*. Draw a picture of the animal you like best. Write the animal's name.
5. Look at the "Three Billy Goats Gruff" filmstrip (uncaptioned). Make up the story and tell it to your class while you show the filmstrip.

Second Grade
1. Look at the *earth globe.* Show somebody where these places are:
   Atlantic Ocean   Pacific Ocean   Which is larger?
   North Pole   South Pole   United States
2. Find the *title* of a book about WHALES. Write the *call number.* Is this a *true* or a *make-believe* book? Write one interesting fact about whales.
3. In a *picture dictionary,* find words that begin with:

wh	fl	spr
wr	gr	tr
th	pl	sw
br	sh	dr
ch	pr	sk

4. Look at *filmstrip* #FS _____ with the title _____ (captioned). Answer these questions in sentences on paper: _____ _____ _____.
5. Find the *call number* for POETRY in the *card catalog.* Find a poem you like in a book. Read it onto a tape. Say or read it to your class.

Third Grade
1. Find the *transparencies* on the life cycle of a frog. Study them. Share the transparencies with your class.
2. Use the box game of *Library Terms.* Match the terms with their meanings.
3. Make a *puppet* of your favorite book character.
4. Find a subject of interest in *The Golden Encyclopedia.* Read it. Draw a picture. Tell your class what you learned.
5. In the *subject* drawer, look up FOLKLORE—GERMANY. Write the *call numbers* and *titles* for several German fairy tale books. Who were the brothers who collected these stories? Check out several books and share them with your class.

If the school library is an exciting place to learn and to enjoy literature, then children have been properly launched in the direction of continuous, rewarding learning.

SCOPE AND SEQUENCE FOR RESEARCH AND REPORTING

Gr.	Search Task	Strategy	Source	Note Taking	Outlining	Bibliographic Form	Reporting
K	Seek simple answers. Compare.	Ask questions. Classify. Browse. Listen. Realia.	*Childcraft.* Study prints. Films. Filmstrips.	What? Why?	Ask related questions.	Recognize source.	Teacher reads. Children interpret words and pictures. Act out. Children answer teacher's analytical, inferential, evaluative questions. Children recognize likenesses and differences.
1	Find words. Find facts.	Use alphabetical order. Recall subject. Ask librarian for help. Recognize call number. Browse in Dewey number section. Browse in book.	Picture dictionary. True books. Pictorial reference works.	What? Where? Recognize and/or dictate answer in sentence.		Use ready reference form. Show material. Tell title. Tell page number.	Recognize meanings. Tell or read answer in sentence.

2	Recall sequence.	Study illustrations. Recognize key word. Use index to: reference set, volume, book. Use numerical order.		Adult records facts in sentence. How?	Put facts in order physically, orally.		Explain sequence. Teacher records various facts in sequence.
	Find meanings.	Use guide words. Recognize glossary. Peruse. Skim. Find key word. Read to find out.	Primary dictionary. Compton's *Precyclopedia*.	What? Who? When?	Rearrange short answers.	Recognize given title. Record page number.	Recall meanings.
	Find related facts.	Use card catalog: drawer labels, guide tabs, subject cards, call numbers. Recognize paragraph, chapter		Use numbered paper or ditoed form. Write short answers. Copy correct spelling. Use neatness.			Write subject heading. Compose written sentences from notes. Proofread and correct. Read sentences orally.

Gr.	Search Task	Strategy	Source	Note Taking	Outlining	Bibliographic Form	Reporting
3	Distinguish dictionary from encyclopedia use. Sequence facts. Draw conclusion.	Distinguish meanings. Use glossary. Use headings. Use subheadings or lead sentences. Use picture captions.	Intermediate dictionary. Glossary. *Golden Encyclopedia.* *World Book Encyclopedia.*	List several facts under each heading. Indent.	Arrange headings beforehand. Number headings.	Record title, page, author on dittoed bibliographic form. Recognize printed bibliography, single bibliographic citation, mediography. Recognize place of publication, publisher, copyright date.	Write meanings. Write headings. Write subheadings in sentences. Compose inferential or evaluative sentence. Read report orally.

Selected Mediography of Library
Skills Teaching Materials

Beck, Margaret V., Vera M. Pace, and Marion L. Welken. *Library Skills: Kindergarten and Primary Grades.* 513-00152-2. Teacher's Manual, $6.95, T.S. Denison & Company.

Beck, Margaret V., Vera M. Pace, and Marion L. Welken. *Library Skills: Book One—Using the Card Catalog.* 513-00153-0. Teacher's Manual, $6.95. Pupil's Workbook—Book One, 513-00154-9, $.65. Spirit Master Workbook—Book One 513-01451-9, $5.95. T.S. Denison & Company, 5100 West 82 Street, Minneapolis, Minnesota 55437.

Craig, Paul M. *Mr. Wiggle's Book* (Book Care). 513-01158-7, $3.50. One book and one cassette 513-06167-3, $7.50. Four books and one cassette 513-06221-1, $14.00. Denison.

Library Angels (Book Care). Four posters (11" x 17") LA-285 $3.00. Sturgis Library Products, Box-130, Sturgis, Michigan 49091.

Library Media Skill Charts. 18 full-color charts (23" x 36"), drilled and eyeletted. Teacher's Manual. ID-2780. Learning World, 500 Westlake Avenue North, Seattle, Washington 98109.

Library Skills for Primary Grades K-3. TDW02, 12 full-color transparencies, 24 duplicating masters, $7.95. DW02, 24 duplicating masters, $3.95. Milliken Publishing, 611 Olive Street, St. Louis, Missouri 63101.

Library Studies, Volume 1, Grades 3-6. Duplicating Masters. #5018, $.25. The Spice Series, Educational Service, Box 219, Stevensville, Michigan 49127.

Using Your Library Posters. 20 full-color (11½" x 16") #150, $6.95. The Instructor Publications, Box 6108, Duluth, Minnesota 55806.

Taking Your Child to the Library

Constance V. Alongi
Brunswick, New Jersey, Public Schools

Women's lib has given today's mother a view of her responsibilities that would have been unheard of years ago. What self-respecting homemaker of past decades, donned in her crisp cotton housedress, would have brooked a reference to her weekly laundering as valet service? Or her loving way with mop, broom, and dust cloth as maid service? Or her skills as meal planner and cook reduced to the level of a scullery maid? Really!

But there is one chore mothers of the past were spared, which is fast becoming one more of many jobs definitely listed under "Mom." The job we refer to is that of chauffeur.

In traveling to and from her several weekly destinations as family chauffeur, today's mother tallies mileage on the car to rival the totals of a traveling salesperson. Besides a regular schedule of grocery shopping; pickup and delivery services; and visits to the dentist, orthodontist, or allergist, she might have to make trips to a bus or train or to school; to music, art, dancing, horseback lessons; and so on, ad infinitum. Is our list complete? No. There's one more place in our suburban society that might require the use of a four-wheeled motor-driven vehicle piloted by our keeper of the car keys.

It's a library. This is one place you can enjoy with your children, affording you a measure of reward in return for your

Reprinted with permission from *The PTA Magazine*, Vol. 67, No. 7.

efforts. In fact, an hour spent in a public library today can actually be therapeutic for a mother! Why not initiate a weekly or biweekly visit to the library as part of your family's activities, to nourish their love of reading as you nourish their bodies?

One librarian sadly reported that the most common reason for a mother's trip to the library with her child is to find material for reports or projects assigned in school. She described a harried mother trailing behind the child, nervously tracking down the right book or encyclopedic reference. Once it has been located, she usually hurries the child along so that she can get on with her other chores. This sort of activity serves little purpose other than annoying the librarian, especially if it is one of several requests to fulfill the same assignment for the same teacher in the same week.

This has been an example of what taking your child to the library should not be: the thwarted use of an enriching facility and a lost opportunity for shared pleasure between you and your child.

What then is the proper use of the library? There are many, ranging from rather casual browsing to definite topical research. But the key to doing it successfully is doing it regularly. When going to the library together becomes a natural facet of your family life, you and your child can share the love of books for recreational purposes and, at the same time, keep abreast of school topics comfortably, at leisure, freeing the librarian to perform tasks that utilize her creativity, not tax her memory of the Dewey Decimal System.

After you have achieved a certain degree of familiarity with your library and its various sections, exploring the bookstacks with your child can be great fun. It is also good practice in alphabetizing, following numerical sequence, and classifying—all skills that are taught in school.

The pleasure of reading aloud may have been obscured in our multimedia world, but its value has never diminished. Regular listening to fluent oral reading at home can be reinforcement of one of the skills your child's teacher hopes to impart, that of using proper phrasing and inflection to enhance comprehension.

The books of Dr. Seuss, Maurice Sendak, and Don Freeman offer many opportunities for delightful sharing with primary grade children. In fact, some of the Seuss rhymes and tongue twisters could constitute a fun approach to phonics drills for children in the middle grades as well. Any book by E.B. White, Roald Dahl, Laura Ingalls Wilder, and Clyde Bulla will be rich in imagery and simulation of detail. Children of middle and intermediate grades adopt them as favorites year after year.

Topical research can be guided by the hobby or current interest of your child: books about sea shells, Indians, prehistoric animals, the history of words—these can be shared by picking specific pertinent passages to read aloud after they have been enjoyed independently.

Looking for books together should be a joyous activity for you and your child, so it is very important that the reading and library going experiences be kept pleasurable and free from stress. Guiding without dominating is the best role to play in this.

If you wish to encourage your child to read, allow him the benefit of reading books of his own choice and his grade level. This will give him practice in easy oral reading, thereby reinforcing the fun of it.

Another approach to sharing fun through books is to look for the lesser known works of famous authors or, conversely, the lesser known authors of famous works.

A journey into any one of the fourteen volume *Land of Oz* series by L. Frank Baum yields a whole world of characters, places, and ideas in which Dorothy and her familiar companions are but secondary characters. These stories are great for vocabulary enrichment and have a gently facetious way of looking at human foibles, providing satire on a level children can understand. And who knows—if children can recognize and enjoy eccentric traits in the characters that people the stories they read, might it not be easier for them to honor diversity among living people? Baum had a great gift for eliciting this spirit in his stories.

Using the library to enrich your children's knowledge about the lesser known works of famous authors can be a bridge to helping them appreciate an author's style before they are afflicted with "classics shock" in junior high school. By familiarizing them early with small, easily assimilated bits of

Shakespeare and Dickens—by reading to them, of course—studying the classics later on will be like meeting old friends.

Granted that much of the language in the classics is of another time, selected paragraphs or poetic speeches can be delightful entities in themselves. An example would be Dickens' description of a dining room closet in *The Mystery of Edwin Drood*: it makes the reader all but able to smell and taste the goodies stored within.

In the same book, Dickens' description of two waiters serving at dinner provides a hilarious study in contrast that is as funny as any TV cartoon. But the mental images are drawn by the reader, not a professional cartoonist, and this, after all, is the very best reason for going to the library and reading with your child: to help him to enjoy his own ability to think and imagine. This may well be the last frontier of individuality.

Never before has it been so urgent for mothers to concern themselves with more than their children's physical welfare. From all directions we are barraged by visual and verbal images not of our own making. We must continuously stoke the fires of curiosity and imagination to prevent their becoming satiated by the ephemeral delights of our visual world.

To do this we must acknowledge the priority of activities that might tax our time and minds, such as getting into the car for the umpteenth time this week and making it to the library, come what may. But in resisting the temptation to succumb wholly to visual media, we will reap dividends of inestimable worth to ourselves, our children, and, ulitmately, society at large.

So go to the library—and enjoy!

Part Two
Involving Children with Literature

Some children read avidly and want nothing more than to be left alone with a book. Other children can become book lovers but require more active experiences in order to discover the joys of reading. Articles in this section suggest ways parents, teachers, and librarians can lead children into books, helping them to appreciate character roles, plots, and delightful writing styles. Several articles also suggest positive ways of using media to interest children in books.

The Monson article describes three kinds of responses to literature and suggests some means of generating those responses through home and school reading activities. The Woodbury article develops more fully the techniques for using choral reading and Readers Theatre to build oral interpretation skills.

Jett-Simpson describes the important role parents can play in establishing a positive attitude toward reading. The article includes numerous activities parents or teachers can carry out with young children. Many good books are recommended for this involvement.

The last two articles—one by Johnson and the other by Sloan, Eisenbarth, and Green—look at some means of using media to involve children with books. The Johnson article is particularly concerned with the use of media and literature to enhance social studies related reading. Sloan, Eisenbarth, and Green present a variety of ideas for coordinating literature, filmstrips, art projects, writing, and videotapes to promote interest in books.

Into a Book and Beyond: Responding to Literature

Dianne Monson
University of Washington

The greatest challenge in teaching reading comes when we try to make certain that the act of reading is valued and enjoyed by each child. Teachers cannot accomplish this alone, nor can parents or librarians. Working together, we have a chance for success in helping children to enter fully into the experience of reading.

Many people would agree that the most important belief elementary teachers can foster in students is the belief that reading is worthwhile. Ideally, that belief stems from a personal need for experiences with books and also from the knowledge that books are a valuable source of information. The well-rounded reader finds both purposes important.

Reading experiences that help children learn to value books and time spent with literature will be most effective when they build knowledge about literature as well as enjoyment of books. Indeed, there are many times when awareness of relationships between characters or events in a book can enhance enjoyment of the story. Experiences which make a story come alive and draw the child into a book can provide the basis for a genuine love of reading.

What are some of the ways in which children and adults respond to literature, and what experiences can help to encourage those responses? Both questions deserve more than a few pages, but the ideas from this article and others in this volume may be useful to teachers, parents, and librarians who have responsibilities for guiding reading inside and outside of school.

Kinds of Responses

No two people are likely to respond in exactly the same way to the same book. Each of us brings a different set of experiences to reading and those experiences influence the way we react to what we read. Certain patterns of response can be observed when children talk or write about what they have read. *Personal response*, indicating that the reader associates with a story character or with some incident in the story, is very important, for it can open the way to other responses. Personal response usually indicates some degree of emotional involvement with the story. The emotional commitment is important. It is probably fair to say that most of us remember best the books we have laughed or cried over or, perhaps, have pondered for some time following the reading. Such books awaken in us a sense that our own hopes, fears, joys, and questions are shared by others.

Personal, or emotional, responses are not by any means the only important ones. Children must be challenged to make sense of what they read. *Interpretive responses* show that they are thinking seriously about what they find in books, learning to infer what a character is like from clues the author gives, knowing when a bit of figurative language must be interpreted as such, being able to generate ideas about happenings not explicit in the plot but necessary to explain an unusual occurrence in the story. These responses form the basis for later, more analytic, study of literature. When a child is emotionally involved with a story, the interpretive response is enriched because the characters and situations seem more vital and believable. Interpretation and ability to react emotionally are at the heart of meaningful and worthwhile reading experiences.

A third kind of response that children should be encouraged to make is the *critical response*. The term is used here to mean ability to evaluate a story or poem, to consider whether the book is good, and to determine the qualities that make it good (in the eyes of the reader). This is not to recommend that we teach literary criticism or close analysis of the text in elementary grades. But it is a suggestion that even kindergartners can begin to make judgments about books in the light of what they enjoy reading. There is value in the experience of trying to explain why a certain character is a favorite or why the book is hard to put down. Guided thinking at early ages may be valuable background for future study of literature. It will certainly help to develop skill in book selection, an ability necessary if children are to establish the habit of library use and keep it into adulthood.

Developing Responsive Readers

In order to create the habit of response that goes beyond literal retelling of a story, we must seek out ways to let children interact with the various elements of a story—the characters, plot structure, setting, even the author's style. If we consider children's book related experiences outside of school, it is clear that oral language and drama are important. They may provide a good bridge to school based experiences with reading. Children are read to by parents, grandparents, older children, or babysitters. The reading may not be professional quality, but the experience is usually one children look forward to. Many children also spend a good deal of time watching television. Although parents and teachers express concern about overuse of television, it is important to realize that not all television fare is unrelated to literature. Some shows are based, however loosely, on books that children can find in the library. They depict, to some extent, development of characters and plots that children find in books. Perhaps the real challenge is to try to compete with television by generating an interest in books as a potential source of dramatic scripts. The visual image intrigues children. At the same time, it removes one of the most natural responses of a reader—the personal visual image of a scene or character. If we are able to help children discover the importance of an author's description as the basis for reproducing a scene, television may be a good medium to develop appreciation for what they read.

If we begin with a dual focus on oral language and on drama, several interesting and useful teaching strategies come to mind. One good idea is to vary the typical situation in which an adult (or older child) reads aloud to a child. In the new version, the responsibility for reading is shared. If several children are involved (as is likely in a classroom or library), each child chooses a character and reads the dialogue parts assigned to that character. If the situation is one adult/one child (as is more common at home), the adult reads the narrational parts and the child reads the dialogue sections. This strategy is effective for developing personal response and interpretation of character traits. It is especially successful if the adult guides children's thinking during prereading time so that they consider carefully what the characters are like. Let them think of the clues the author gives about characters. What words would they use to describe each character? How would the characters probably talk? What emotions would they show? Using that information, children can give a well thought out interpretation of the dialogue. The technique provides background for appreciating the means by which an author can use description as well as dialogue to give information about characters.

An activity that builds on children's experiences with television and their love of action is dramatization of an episode from a book. The dramatization can actually be carried out or it can take the form of planning an adaptation from book to television drama. In any event, the planning must occur first if the dramatization is to be successful.

Reconstructing a story for dramatization requires careful thinking about the characters, setting, and plot. What scene or scenes would be good ones to dramatize? Who are the characters necessary to stage a scene that has been selected? What are their most striking traits? What good and bad qualities do they seem to have? How might they walk? talk? behave towards one another? Does each character behave in the same way throughout the scene? In what ways does a character change? Children may not agree with one another as they try to describe the characters, and the disagreements may call for rereading of sections of the story. Minor differences in opinion are likely to persist, however, and they may be attributed to the fact that each reader brings a different set of experiences to the interpretation of a story. It is important to discuss that notion with children, emphasizing the fact that we must respect our own opinions and also those of others.

Questions can help children to think about important aspects of the plot, too. What incidents are most important in the scene? In what order do they occur? How does the action lead from one incident to the next? What characters will be needed for each incident that is included in the scene? The analysis that goes into planning a dramatization gives experience in looking at plot from the standpoint of sequence of events and the means by which they are related.

Setting is important to any dramatization, and description of setting is an important aspect of good writing. Children may enjoy trying to design a set that could be used for the scene they have selected, sketching the set or actually building it as a model. To do this, they will have to reread carefully, paying attention to descriptive phrases the author uses. They may also be interested in thinking back through an entire book to list the various settings that would be needed for a filmed version of the book. The next step would be to list terms and phrases used by the author to describe each scene. Finally, the scenes can be drawn and colored or painted and displayed on a bulletin board. The outcome may lead to a discussion of the author's style, paying particular attention to the interpretation of the descriptive phrases. Comparison of attempts by several children to illustrate scenes, using information from the story, will also underscore the differences in personal responses to books. These differences should always be treated so that they are accepted by the children as well as the teacher.

If the planned dramatization is produced, children have the added experience of trying out the character roles—being the character as well as trying to remember and reproduce the incidents accurately so as to make the scene effective. Such a dramatization takes considerable time to prepare but, when the book or scene is well chosen, it can be very satisfying to all involved.

Questions can be used effectively to help children perceive a story from the inside rather than the outside, as a spectator, particularly when the questions make children curious about the feelings of story characters. This can be effectively accomplished by the use of point-of-view questioning techniques (1). Instead of asking children why they think a character, such as Ramona in *Ramona the Pest*, thought she would get a present during her first day of school, phrase it this way: "You are Ramona. Why did you think you would get a present that first day of kindergarten?" The key to this form of questioning is to phrase the questions so that children must answer as though they were one of the characters. Asking questions such as "How did you feel when you finally learned to whistle?" (*Whistle for Willy*) or "Why did you enjoy living alone for an entire winter?" (*My Side of the Mountain*) can enable children to perceive characters more fully and to verbalize some of the emotional reactions they may have experienced during the reading.

Children who are able to respond emotionally to what they read and to make sense of a story by using their own experiences to interpret language, actions, and characterization are on the way to becoming habitual readers. These are the children who constantly hound the librarian for more books by a favorite author and wait for new books to arrive. Such children may be reading critically, learning to know and value the books that give them the greatest satisfaction. Most children, however, need guidance in knowing what makes a book good and in deciding which books they would place in that category. It is not suggested here that a set of criteria or a list of "good books" would be the same for all children. However, children can benefit from the experience of making judgments about books.

The business of children's evaluation of books has been introduced successfully in a project cosponsored by IRA and the Children's Book Council. Children from a number of school districts throughout the country have participated in the project annually since it began in 1974. Each year, publishers are invited to submit recently published books that children will react to. Five teams of educators, located in five different geographic areas, are responsible for getting the books into the hands of children and for keeping track of their reactions to the books. As many as 400 or 500 books may be included in one year. Children are asked to respond to questions and other formats designed by participating teachers. Some representative questions are: "Is this one of the best books you have read? How does the book compare with your favorite books? Should it be in our school library? Would your friends enjoy reading it?

What did you like best about the book?" These and other questions help children to get at a critical judgment of each story. Teachers and librarians working with the project have noticed that children often have a hard time when they first begin the process, tending to think that most of the books are good and giving no sound reasons for the judgment. At best, very general reasons such as "I just like it" are given at first. As they profit from teacher guidance and become more experienced, however, children are able to differentiate more easily between books they value and those they do not. They are also more able to give logical reasons for their judgments. The results of the yearly project have been published each autumn in *The Reading Teacher* under the title "Classroom Choices," listing the favorite books.

The activities described here are some ways to enlarge children's experiences with books so their responses will include emotional reaction as well as interpretive and critical reactions. As children are able to respond more fully to various aspects of literature, they will be moving toward the ability to make thoughtful selections of books they choose to read. Parents, librarians, and teachers working together can help to make that goal a reality.

Reference
1. Sebesta, Sam Leaton. "The Neglected Art: Thought Questions," *Elementary English*, December 1967.

Choral Reading and Readers Theatre: Oral Interpretation of Literature in the Classroom

Jean Woodbury
Educational Consultant

Have you ever found a poem or a story so appealing that you wished you could share it with your class, but you didn't quite know how to go about it? You had recently read one or two poems to your students and didn't want to overdo it. Besides, you were already involved in reading fifteen minutes daily from a classic children's story—one that might be too difficult for some of the children to read for themselves but which enthralled them when you read it to them.

No, the story or poem you wanted to share was not difficult. It may even have been easy reading for your group. But past experience with handing copies of such a poem or story to the children and asking them to read silently so they could share their responses had not been encouraging. Somehow the excitement evaporated in the exercise.

If the next time you find such a poem or story you find words and phrases frequently heard in everyday conversation, think about using oral interpretation—the children's own oral interpretation—to bring the literature alive. Two forms of oral interpretation that are fun to do and are intellectually stimulating can be readily handled in the classroom. You can call them reading or language arts—they are both. And if you use one or both forms occasionally, you'll be sure to have a group of children who have grown in their love for and understanding of some subtleties of our language. These forms are choral reading (which usually requires poetry) and Readers Theatre (which makes use of prose and, sometimes, poetry).

The poem that lends itself to choral reading has good but not overpowering rhythm, some alliteration or onomatopoeia, and words or phrases that are either humorous or sound like something you've read at home. The poem probably has images that remind you and the children of common experiences or feelings. The story that best lends itself to Readers Theatre treatment is relatively short, uses language that your students can read with ease, has a simple and obvious story line, and contains dialogue that can be "played" by individual students. A strong thread of humor or drama or pathos is necessary. And, as in poems for choral reading, the phraseology should be the kind children have heard either in their own homes or in the old, oral tradition. This doesn't mean that the literature should not contain any new or idiosyncratic language. It just means that children should be able to put themselves into the story, either through firsthand experience or through imaginative experiences they have gained from folklore, fairy tales, reading, radio, and television.

You may have wondered sometimes, as I have, why certain stories and poems lend themselves to silent reading and enjoyment and others come alive only when read aloud or performed. The answer probably lies in the essentially oral nature of the language in these latter pieces of literature as compared with the conventional language commonly used in written literature. In a recently proposed theory of language development integrating the notion of meaning as external to language (utterances) with the notion of meaning as intrinsic to language (text), Olson (4) mentions drama and poetry as literary forms which, although printed, are oral in their nature and depend for their effect on the mediation of a shared oral tradition. The poems we select for choral reading and the plays or stories we choose for Readers Theatre have large components of words, phrases, and dialogues borrowed directly from speech patterns. It stands to reason, then, that they are enjoyed most when interpreted orally.

What follows are two summaries of some principles of selection, preparation, presentation, and benefits to be derived from the use of choral reading and Readers Theatre in the classroom. A short bibliography suggests resources for learning about and getting materials for these oral activities.

Woodbury

Choral Reading

Four principles for selecting poems to be read in chorus are sufficient:

1. Make it relatively short.
2. Keep it simple. The reading level should be no higher than that of the poorer readers in your group, preferably somewhat below the group's instructional level. Choose material at the independent reading level.
3. Look for something with a catchy title that will put imaginations to work.
4. Select a poem that will come alive when read aloud— words with fascinating sounds, contrast of some sort that can be interpreted, mood that can be enhanced through oral interpretation, or dialogue that bears the stamp of personality.

Preparation for choral reading can be guided by one principle—contrast. Your medium is a group of voices. Therefore it's useful to have one or two simple classifications for the voices in your class—high and low, for instance, as well as strong and soft. Of course, these basic voice tendencies can and should be extended, but it may be wise to begin with what the children produce naturally and work gradually for more range.

Some elements of contrast you may choose to work with are

1. Low voice versus high voice.
2. One voice versus two or more voices.
3. Small group versus large group.
4. Mixed voices versus high or low voices.
5. Fast delivery versus slow or moderate delivery.
6. Smooth flowing versus punctuated or choppy delivery.
7. Aggressive versus unctious delivery.
8. One line versus many lines.

You can and will think of other elements of contrast.

In building your interpretation on these constrasts, you and your students will note some subtleties of our language are enhanced through oral rendition—such things as onomato-poeia, alliteration, rhythm, unusual and interesting phrases, and words that invoke connotations. This is part of what makes choral reading fun. You, as teacher, need not be the only person to have ideas for playing with words and phrasing. In fact, if right from the start you allow your students to make suggestions for interpretation, and you let the group try out their suggestions to see what the sound is, your students will find choral reading twice as much fun. And it's almost certain that you will be surprised at the inventiveness of your students, as well as their good judgment in selecting which interpreta-tion they like best.

You may wonder who is to be the audience for the choral reading. The answer is, your own group. The process of trying out different interpretations and deciding which to use automatically calls for self-monitoring. It is this process that educates the child—and you. You can expect growth in your students in their abilities to cooperate in planning and interpreting a piece of literature. You can expect your students to become more aware of the nuances in meaning, sound, and rhythm to be found in poetry. And you can help them see that language is sometimes a toy to be played with, a toy that requires the imagination and cooperation of their classmates to work. Choral reading is a cooperative project. The bonus for the reading teacher is the natural forum it provides for allowing students to read aloud without the embarrassment of being individually judged on performance. Even the child who has a solo line has the support of the whole group in planning for its delivery.

Let the decision to perform for another audience evolve naturally—if it does. Choral reading is like creative dramatics in this respect. Its value is largely in the growth that occurs with practice. If another class wants to hear you interpret a poem, fine! Accept the invitation with pleasure and make the reading a gift to them. Enjoy it when you perform and don't worry about perfection. Then, when your class is ready to try choral reading on another poem, you can have another good time playing with the language.

Woodbury

Readers Theatre

Readers Theatre is an art form not so widely known and certainly not so widely used as choral reading in the classroom. Coger and White (*3*) define Readers Theatre as follows: "Basically, Readers Theatre is a medium in which two or more oral interpreters through their oral reading cause an audience to experience literature." They further explain that "the essence of Readers Theatre is creative oral reading which calls forth mental images of characters enacting a scene that exists primarily in the minds of the participants—both the readers' and the audience's."

With or without a narrator, Readers Theatre participants establish the focus of the piece not onstage but in the imaginations of the listeners. Exposition does not lend itself to this treatment. But a reading of Browning's "Pied Piper of Hamelin," with the readers taking the parts of the Mayor, the Piper, and the Little Lame Boy, would be Readers Theatre if the locus was not onstage but in the imaginations of the audience.

Certain conventions, listed below, surround Readers Theatre. In the classroom it is wise to start by adhering to these conventions completely so as to experience the art form as it is intended. After class and teacher become familiar with the techniques, there may be occasions when you would want to involve the students who are acting as audience in some ritualized or crowd responses. For instance, "The Reluctant Dragon" by Kenneth Grahame, adapted for Readers Theatre by Glynn and Coger, has several instances when the townspeople shout something together. This provides a good opportunity for students not involved in reading the parts of the characters to get into the act. It's fun.

Readers Theatre requires that the narrator and readers form a group seated in front of an audience. The arrangement of the group can vary, but you'll probably have a consensus about who should sit where. The grouping can be made more visually exciting through use of stools varying in height, or of platforms on which stools or chairs can be placed.

Among the conventions—things to do and not to do— usually honored in Readers Theatre are:

1. Scenery and costumes are not used or they are only selectively employed.
2. Action or physical movement is merely suggested by the interpreter and is visualized in the minds of the audience.
3. A narrator, speaking directly to the audience, usually establishes the basic situation or theme and links the various segments together.
4. A physical script is usually carried by the reader or at least is in evidence somewhere.
5. There is a continuing effort to develop and maintain a closer, more personalized relationship between performer and audience—a relationship requiring a different kind of participation from that demanded in conventional theatre. In Readers Theatre, the emphasis is on aural appeal and the audience's attention is concentrated on the literature. The meaning underlying the words is shared with the audience.

Although this art form and the conventions surrounding it were developed with theatre presentations in mind, the form is usable in the classroom and allows for much the same kind of growth as does choral reading. It builds on dramatic prose with dialogue, rather than poetry, however; and it requires more sustained individual interpretation than does choral reading. In addition, seldom would a whole class fit into a Readers Theatre presentation. Instead, a small group within a class would plan, practice, and present a reading. The total class could be involved if two or three scripts were rehearsed concurrently. Then a day could be set aside when groups perform for each other.

An unfortunate fact about Readers Theatre scripts should be stated right now. There are not many published or at least I have not been able to find many. The best source I know is Coger and White's *Readers Theatre Handbook: A Dramatic Approach to Literature* (3). There are several good scripts in the book appropriate for use in secondary schools but too difficult for the elementary grades. A teacher interested in trying Readers Theatre in the classroom might find it both fun and informative to gather together a group of adult friends to read one of these scripts. If you do this, you'll see what the possibilities are at the grade level you teach. The next thing to do is to develop one or two scripts of your own from an appropriate story. I've seen scripts developed from Kipling's *Elephant Child* and O'Henry's *Ransom of Red Chief.* I developed a script almost word for word from *Frog and Toad Together* by Arnold Lobel. Don't let the lack of scripts deter you. Get the students in your class involved in searching for short stories that can be turned into scripts. Stories aimed at readers younger than themselves might be best. Perhaps some of your students would turn these stories into scripts for you. You can see the possibilities in this activity for crossing the borders between reading and language arts.

Some of the values to be derived from Readers Theatre, according to Coger and White, are:

1. Vitalized literary study

Alfred North Whitehead, in discussing the aims of education, said, "Above all, the art of reading aloud should be cultivated." Coger and White say that Readers Theatre is a means "whereby students can be influenced not only to love good literature but also to become tremendously excited about it, to analyze the meanings and style with avid interest, to want to share their enthusiasm with other students and with parents and friends" (*3*).

2. Personal development

Coger and White state: "Since the readers have only their voices, the muscle tone of their bodies, and their facial expressions by which to convey the ideas, the emotions, and the attitudes expressed in the literature, they are motivated to develop rich, flexible, expressive voices and to free themselves from muscular tensions so that they can respond vocally and physically to the content of the literary material."

3. Cultural enrichment

It is possible for an interpreter to read aloud many plays for which a fully staged production would be too costly, or to read aloud individual scenes as students study plays in class. In fact, the medium can make use of the entire literary spectrum—poetry, narratives, letters, diaries, biographies, and other forms of literature, as well as plays.

In the elementary classroom, Readers Theatre emphasis almost certainly would be on narratives or simple plays. But a tremendous potential for growth in reading, literature appreciation, and love for the English language is present in the use of Readers Theatre in the classroom.

References
1. Arbuthnot, Mary Hill, et al. *The Arbuthnot Anthology of Literature*, Fourth Edition (revised by Zena Sutherland). Palo Alto, California: Scott, Foresman, 1976.
2. Arbuthnot, Mary Hill, and Shelton L. Root, Jr. *Time for Poetry*, Third General Edition. Palo Alto, California: Scott, Foresman, 1968.
3. Coger, Leslie Irene, and Melvin R. White. *Readers Theatre Handbook: A Dramatic Approach to Literature*. Glenview, Illinois: Scott, Foresman, 1968.
4. Olson, David R. "From Utterance to Text: The Bias of Language in Speech and Writing," *Harvard Educational Review*, August 1978, 258.

Parents and Teachers Share Books with Young Children

Mary Jett-Simpson
University of Wisconsin at Milwaukee

Parents are the most important resource for developing readiness for formal reading instruction. Parents can establish an attitude toward reading by giving books an important place in their own daily lives as well as in the lives of their children. Fathers and mothers who sit down regularly to read magazines, newspapers, and books communicate to their children that reading is valuable and esteemed. Because of the strong emotional ties between parents and children, children usually seek to emulate their parents. Parents have the power of their actions. Children want to do as Mom and Dad do. Thus the children are eager to have parents share with them that which they treasure, books.

Parents have a deceptively simple but powerful sharing technique available to them. It is the "lap technique." It involves setting aside twenty to thirty minutes each evening for curling up in a comfortable chair or couch with their child or children nestled on their laps or snuggled close. As children sit safely and securely in this loving environment, the stories and poems shared with them take on greater importance. Many of us as adults can think back to stories which are favorites because they were shared with us in this way.

Parents can deeply enrich the book sharing experience by selecting a variety of books and expanding their strategies for sharing these books. In the remainder of this paper I will suggest types of books appropriate for sharing with young children and techniques for sharing them. The ideas presented are applicable in the home and best implemented through the lap technique. With slight modification, the ideas can also be used by teachers in nursery schools, kindergartens, and primary grades.

Books for Sharing

Mother Goose is a must. The rhyme and rhythm of the poems enchant the children. After repeated exposure, children can be heard chanting these communicable rhymes to their dolls or trucks during play. There is a delightful assortment of Mother Goose books available. They range from the classically illustrated book *The Mother Goose Treasury (2)* to the contemporary illustrations in *Brian Wildsmith's Mother Goose (40)*. Variety of exposure will increase the children's appreciation of the unique forms of illustrations. Of course, very young children should have the little cloth Mother Goose books. Mother Goose favorites should be read over and over so they are naturally committed to memory. At that point, it is fun to play a game of "fractured nursery rhymes" with the children. This is done by saying a familiar rhyme and purposely substituting a wrong rhyming word. For example: "Hickory dickory dock, the mouse ran up the elephant." As the children correct the adult, they are showing sensitivity to the rhyme form as well as the content of the poems. That is part of auditory discrimination discussed frequently in reading readiness materials.

Alphabet books are important books for early sharing experiences. Some of these are presented in rhyme such as *Ape in a Cape: An Alphabet of Odd Animals (4)*. Some use marvelously large words as in *As I Was Crossing the Boston Common (6)*, and others are very simple. A book that will delight many children is *ABC Science Experiments (28)*. For each object named for each letter of the alphabet, a simple experiment is described. For example:

J   jet
Make a jet flyer.
Blow up a long balloon.

Let go of it.
What does the
balloon do?

Not only will children begin to learn to name and visually discriminate letters, they will also have opportunities to add words to their vocabulary and extend thoughts about their environment. When sharing these books, parents and teachers can encourage their children to name the letters as they turn the pages and name the item presented in the pictures. They can also encourage them to repeat rhymes and phrases.

Excursions to the grocery store, which are weekly events for most families, can sometimes result in discoveries at the children's book counter. One such discovery was *There's A Monster at the End of This Book (33)*. Who can resist turning the pages of the book when lovable, furry old Grover says "Shhhh. Listen, I have an idea. If you do not turn any pages, we will never get to the end of this book. And that is good, because there is a MONSTER at the end of this book. So please do not turn the page." When reading the book aloud, it is fun to increase the suspense by pretending to put the book away so that no one has to see the terrifying monster at the end of the book. Naturally, the child will be begging the reader to continue. The reader could make the story even more exciting by varying the pitch of the voice to reflect Grover's emotions. Children like to have stories read aloud to them in excited voices *(29)*.

As the author of *There's A Monster at the End of This Book* develops the story, he involves the children with some concepts necessary to understanding how a book "works"; for example, front to back orientation and left to right sequencing. In *Would You Like to Play Hide and Seek in This Book with Lovable, Furry Old Grover? (34)*, additional book orientation concepts such as tops and bottoms of pages are developed in the same appealing Sesame Street style. On the surface, orienting a book appears simple; to the experienced book handler, it is. However, children with no book experience can be readily identified in a group of children who have had experience. They can be seen to flounder through books, sometimes going backwards and right to left. Children must know how to handle a book and understand basic book organization as a prerequisite to formal reading instruction.

Basic concept books such as those by Tana Hoban expand children's understandings of relationships in their own world. *Push Pull, Empty Full* (12) develops the concept of opposites through superb black and white photographs with sensitive eye appeal. *Circles, Triangles, and Squares* (13), *Over, Under, and Through* (14), *Shapes and Things* (15), and *Count and See* (16), all by Hoban, take the child on a photographic exploration of concepts. Children, and parents as well, will be particularly enchanted with *Look Again* (17) in which the viewer first sees a picture of part of an object through a small square hole on a blank page. It is like looking through a small window. It is the children's challenge to guess what the whole thing could be, hidden behind the cutout page. After guessing, the page can be turned to expose the complete picture of the object.

Easy to read books are readily available to parents and teachers. Dr. Suess (Theodor Geisel) has become a household favorite through the rhymes and antics of characters such as Sam in *Green Eggs and Ham* (9) and the cat in *The Cat in the Hat* (10). Children love to hear these stories over and over to the extent that they begin to memorize parts and simulate reading by themselves. They know the story so well that they actually appear to be reading it as they synchronize the turning of the pages with their recitation of the story. The story becomes theirs. Children also begin to develop a basic sight vocabulary as well as a strong sense of rhythm and rhyme from these stories.

Stories with cumulative structures are excellent for sharing with children. As these stories build, first one character appears and then another, and another, and so on. In *Ask Mr. Bear* (7), Danny wants to obtain a birthday present for his mother. First he asks the hen, who cannot help him; but the hen goes along with him to ask the next character, a goose. The goose can't help him either but wants to go along. "So Danny and the Hen and the Goose all hopped along until they met...." As this line is repeated in the story with the addition of each new character, it is a perfect time to invite the child to chime in with the reading. This is a good way to involve the child in responding to the sequence of the story as well. It also is interesting for the child to try to guess what the next animal will be and then turn the page to see if he is right.

"Cats here, cats there, cats and kittens everywhere, Hundreds of cats, Thousands of cats, Millions and billions and trillions of cats" is a refrain repeated in the story *Millions of Cats (8)*. When refrains and repeated phrases appear in stories, parents and teachers should pause a moment to cue the child to join in with the reading of the story by repeating the refrain or phrase with them. In many cases, this allows the children to try on new sentence structures which help them expand their facilities with language and acquire new vocabulary. Researchers have found a positive relationship between language and exposure to reading materials in the home *(3)*.

Many children's authors know that children love to play the guessing game. What can it be? What will happen next? Two excellent books that encourage the children to predict are *Rosie's Walk (18)* and *Elephant Buttons (36)*. Rosie, the hen, is being chased by a fox who has chicken dinner on his mind. Each time he is ready to pounce on Rosie there are clues in the picture about what is going to happen to the fox next. Children will enjoy guessing what will happen before turning the page. Usually, they are able to guess correctly and feel particularly smug when they turn the page to see they are correct. In *Elephant Buttons*, the first picture is of an immense elephant with buttons on his belly. What will be on the next page? A horse emerging from the unbuttoned elephant is followed by a horse standing with buttons on his belly. What will emerge from the horse? Well guess first, then turn the page and see.

As parents and teachers search for good stories containing rhyme or cumulative structure or repetition or guessing games, they will often find these elements combined in a single book. Such is the case in Raskin's *Who, Said Sue, Said Whoo? (30)*. The story begins with a cow hiding in a cornfield and a little girl turning to say, "Who said Moo?" When the page is turned for the answer, the cow comes out of hiding and the next sound is heard. "The polka dot cow said moo. Then who, said Sue, said chitter-chitter-chatter, and who said whoo?" The story is also a guessing game as the reader or listener tries to figure out who makes the sound and will be added to the group of congregating creatures.

Techniques for Sharing

Once children have learned to listen to stories, they will delight in creating their own stories to accompany the illustrations in the many charming wordless picture books available. I observed a five year old sitting with a tape recorder, microphone in hand, for one hour telling an elaborate story for *Shrewbettina's Birthday* (11). When she was finished with the telling, she replayed her story and listened as she turned the pages of the wordless picture book. It was clear from her storytelling that she knew how a story developed. She gave her characters life and animation through conversation and action. The personalities were further developed through her description of their emotions and thoughts. Frequently, a child's telling of a story for a wordless picture book incorporates bits of story plot or language borrowed from a story the child has heard, showing that stories are becoming part of his/her daily life. It is motivating, but not necessary, to use a tape recorder for storytelling. Wordless picture books can be shared simply by having the child tell the story to the parent or teacher. Children may enjoy alternating the telling with the adult page by page. A lively dimension can be given to the experience by giving the characters conversation. Wordless picture books by Mercer Mayer have been very popular with children. In a number of his books, a frog is featured as the main character. The mischevious and loving behavior of the frog portrayed through the animated, humorous illustrations is especially captivating in *A Boy, A Dog, and A Frog* (25), *Frog On His Own* (26), and *Frog Goes to Dinner* (27).

Realistic stories allow children to relate their own personal experiences to the characters in the books. Sometimes the result is that the children are better able to understand themselves, to develop empathy for others and to cope with problems. The good writers of realistic stories first develop a solid story which can stand on its own merit. The story should not be subservient to a didactic message. The story is primary. There are numerous books relating to children's life experiences. For example, if a child is moving, reading *Glad Day, Sad Day* (35) may help the child to better understand the mixed feelings aroused about leaving a familiar place and going to a new one. *Spectacles* will tantalize any reader and particularly those who are getting their first pair of glasses. Staying overnight with a friend for the first time can sometimes be very difficult, as Ira finds out in *Ira Sleeps Over* (38). When a child's pet dies, it is a particularly sad time. Parents and children will find *The Tenth Good Thing about Barney* (30) a comforting story for coping with such an event. After reading books such as these aloud to children, they may wish to talk informally about the experience in the story. Parents and teachers who are unfamiliar with children's book titles relating to a specific theme will find the librarian an invaluable resource person for locating additional books.

As our society shifts its traditional views of men and women so, too, does the world of children's books reflect the changes. Children can now meet characters such as Tulip, an aggressive little girl raccoon who picks fights with timid Benjamin in *Benjamin and Tulip* (39). Their conflict is momentarily abated in the conclusion. Zolotow introduces the reader to a boy who wants a doll for a toy in a sensitive story titled *William's Doll* (41). Such books can help children be less stereotypical in their views of men and women in our culture. In addition, the numerous multiethnic books can serve to illustrate to children the multifaceted nature of our peoples. Books by Ezra Jack Keats tell of universal childhood experiences. In *Goggles* (19) an innercity serves as the backdrop for a conflict between the "big boys" and the "little boys" over a pair of goggles. The little boys are the winners with the help of a resourceful dachshund named Willie. The warm family relationship portrayed in the poetic book, *Black is Brown is Tan* (1), is a strong, positive statement about the supportive interactions among the members of a minority family. *Stevie* (32) and *Nine Days to Christmas* (5) are both powerful stories which give insight into multiethnic groups as well as the universal qualities of peoples. Simply exposing children to multiethnic books has been found to increase positive attitudes toward minorities (20).

Nonfiction books are frequently overlooked for sharing with children. Yet children are fascinated about the world around them. There are excellent books written simply and accurately with clear illustrations which will satisfy children's curiosity about their world as well as raise new questions. What allows us to stand upright? *The Skeleton Book (21)* shows clear x-ray like pictures of animal and human bone structure. *A Drop of Blood (31)*, a book in the Let's Read and Find Out Science Series, gives insight into the importance of blood in a simple and understandable way. These books open doors to discussion and further development of children's curiosity about their world. Some children become intrigued with one topic and find out all they can about it, becoming miniexperts. These children will enjoy talking about their new understandings.

Children deserve the very best children's literature has to offer. The Caldecott Medal books and honor books are a constant source of superior quality. These are books selected on a yearly basis for their excellence in illustrations. A special favorite of young children is the 1971 honor book, *Frog and Toad are Friends (22)*. The tender affection between these friends is underscored by the gentle illustrations of Arnold Lobel. Children who fall in love with these characters will enjoy reading about their further adventures in *Frog and Toad Together (23)* and *Frog and Toad All Year (24)*. Reading aloud excellent books such as these to children in a caring way will capture their imaginations and emotions and develop positive attitudes which will support a lifetime of reading.

References
1. Adoff, Arnold. *Black is Brown is Tan.* New York: Harper and Row, 1973.
2. Briggs, Raymond. *The Mother Goose Treasury.* New York: Coward, McCann, 1966.
3. Chomsky, Carol. "Stages in Language Development and Reading Exposure," *Harvard Educational Review, 43* (1972), 1-33.
4. Eichenberg, Fritz. *Ape in a Cape: An Alphabet of Odd Animals.* New York: Harcourt Brace Jovanovich, 1952.
5. Ets, Marie Hall, and Aurora Labastida. *Nine Days to Christmas.* New York: Viking, 1959.
6. Farber, Norma. *As I Was Crossing the Boston Common.* Illustrated by Arnold Lobel. New York: Dutton, 1973.
7. Flack, Marjorie. *Ask Mr. Bear.* New York: Macmillan, 1932.
8. Gag, Wanda. *Millions of Cats.* New York: Coward, McCann, 1928.
9. Geisel, Theodor. *Green Eggs and Ham.* New York: Random House, 1960.
10. Geisel, Theodor. *The Cat in the Hat.* New York: Random House, 1957.

11. Goodall, John. *Shrewbettina's Birthday*. New York: Harcourt Brace Jovanovich, 1971.
12. Hoban, Tana. *Push Pull, Empty Full*. New York: Macmillan, 1972.
13. Hoban, Tana. *Circles, Triangles, and Squares*. New York: Macmillan, 1974.
14. Hoban, Tana. *Over, Under, and Through*. New York: Macmillan, 1973.
15. Hoban, Tana. *Shapes and Things*. New York: Macmillan, 1970.
16. Hoban, Tana. *Count and See*. New York: Macmillan, 1972.
17. Hoban, Tana. *Look Again*. New York: Macmillan, 1971.
18. Hutchins, Pat. *Rosies Walk*. New York: Macmillan, 1968.
19. Keats, Ezra Jack. *Goggles*. New York: Macmillan, 1969.
20. Litcher, John, and David Johnson. "Changes in Attitudes toward Negroes of White Elementary School Students after Use of Multiethnic Readers," *Journal of Educational Psychology, 60* (1969), 148-152.
21. Livoudais, Madiline, and Robert Dunne. *The Skeleton Book*. New York: Scholastic, 1972.
22. Lobel, Arnold. *Frog and Toad are Friends*. New York: Harper and Row, 1970.
23. Lobel, Arnold. *Frog and Toad Together*. New York: Harper and Row, 1971.
24. Lobel, Arnold. *Frog and Toad All Year*. New York: Harper and Row, 1976.
25. Mayer, Mercer. *A Boy, A Dog, and A Frog*. New York: Dial Press, 1967.
26. Mayer, Mercer. *Frog On His Own*. New York: Dial Press, 1972.
27. Mayer, Mercer. *Frog Goes to Dinner*. New York: Dial Press, 1974.
28. Milgrom, Harry. *ABC Science Experiments*. New York: Collier Books, 1970.
29. Milwaukee Area Right to Read Reading Council Committee. "Teacher Activities and Enrichment Ideas for Motivating Children to Read," *The MARC, 2* (1976), 9-20.
30. Raskin, Ellen. *Who, Said Sue, Said Whoo?* New York: Atheneum, 1973.
31. Showers, Paul. *A Drop of Blood*. Illustrated by Don Madden. New York: Crowell, 1967.
32. Steptoe, John. *Stevie*. New York: Harper and Row, 1969.
33. Stone, Jon. *There's a Monster at the End of This Book*. Illustrated by Mike Smollen. Western Publishing, 1971.
34. Stone, Jon. *Would You Like to Play Hide and Seek in this Book with Lovable, Furry Old Grover?* Illustrated by Mike Smollen. New York: Random House, 1976.
35. Thompson, Vivian. *Glad Day, Sad Day*. Illustrated by Lilian Obligado. New York: Scholastic, 1971.
36. Ueno, Nariko. *Elephant Buttons*. New York: Harper and Row, 1973.
37. Viorst, Judith. *The Tenth Good Thing about Barney*. New York: Atheneum, 1971.
38. Waber, Bernard. *Ira Sleeps Over*. New York: Houghton Mifflin, 1971.
39. Wells, Rosemary. *Benjamin and Tulip*. New York: Dial Press, 1973.
40. Wildsmith, Brian. *Brian Wildsmith's Mother Goose*. New York: Watts, 1964.
41. Zolotow, Charlotte. *William's Doll*. New York: Harper and Row, 1972.

Using Media to Turn Kids on to Reading in the Content Areas

Roger E. Johnson
University of South Florida

There are many reasons that children are having trouble reading and are not reading very much, if at all. The main "reasons" for this situation are that we now live in a nonreading society, television has taken the place of reading and most other activities, and the "back-to-basics" movement is overstressing skills and drills. Our problem is how to get children interested in books and libraries.

Years ago the reading of a book was the highlight of a day because it offered a great deal of enjoyment, excitement, and escape. Regardless of economic class, social status, race, or sex, readers could live in a castle in Camelot, run down the yellow brick road with Dorothy, tame a cattle town with Wyatt Earp, or fall in love with the person of their dreams.

We live in a society that is slowly becoming a nonreading group of more than 200 million people. Thousands of books are published every year but they are being read by only a few people. There are many things to do other than taking the time to read. Nonreading has become such a habit that when we are hungry while driving, we don't even take time to read signs, we just look for the "Golden Arches."

Televison is the main barrier against developing a love for reading. Many articles and books have been written about the effect television has on our society. A summary of all these efforts shows that the main advantages for the TV viewer are that it can be watched in the comfort of one's home and there is no need to get fortified for a December Minnesota Vikings football game. By turning a dial a person can have instantaneous entertainment, if he considers watching "Lucy" or the "Six Million Dollar Man" entertaining. There is constant excitement (the Dingbat got a job), suspense (will the Bionic Woman burn out a transistor?), and sex (will Farrah Fawcett-Majors get another chill?).

The main danger of television addiction is that people can watch thousands of hours of TV without ever having to think. All that is required is for a person to be able to turn a dial, sit, occasionally take a break for a snack, and turn off the set before going to sleep. Not one minute of thinking is required.

The last reason to be considered here as to why people do not read is the growing movement labeled "back-to-basics." This has almost as many definitions as exponents, but it usually refers to stressing the fundamental skills in "reading, writing, and 'rithmetic." To accomplish this, school districts are telling (or forcing) teachers to spend more time teaching these three subjects and to stress skills. The consequences of some of these efforts are that other subject areas are neglected and children are spending so much time on skill, drill, skill, drill that they do not want to read anything. And that is the problem! How do we get children (in all grades) turned on to wanting to read for indepth information, fun, or escape, not only in schools but outside as well?

If we could get the complete cooperation of teachers, librarians, parents, students, Madison Avenue, and so called "stars," it would be easy. We can't simply say "Turn off TV and read, read, read." Teachers and librarians must develop ways to get students turned on to books and resource materials. Therefore, let's take a look at some things that *might* help a teacher get students to read something other than a textbook.

Use cartoons. It is amazing, but we educators are finally realizing that children love cartoons. Children should! Most cartoons are funny, many deal with real life situations, and they usually have only one point to make. So, use them on bulletin boards, assume the roll of a cartoon character when making assignments, or let the students make reports in the form of cartoons (7).

Children are interested in people and they have their heroes, stars, and favorite people. Teachers also like to have students do reports about people who have done things related to what is being studied. However, when many students work on their reports they use a handy encyclopedia and end up writing a "conception to resurrection" biography, beginning with, "So and so was born..." and ending with "...died on September 28, 1932."

Below are some examples of questions you could select to help students zero in on specific parts of a person's life. Hopefully, this would require them to read more than just an encyclopedia. These can be used to report on anyone, including George Washington, Jimmy Carter, or Farrah Fawcett-Majors. But, there is one problem with using these kinds of questions. In a sense, this method is using reading to try to influence more reading. Other things can and should be used, and several suggestions are listed. Although all of the examples deal with Abraham Lincoln, they could be applied to almost anyone in any content area.

Questions like these might be interesting for your children to pursue:

1. Are there any things in your own life which are similar to his/hers?
2. For what things did you admire him/her most?
3. Have you known any other adults who have these qualities?
4. What exactly did he/she achieve?
5. Were his/her goals or aims at all like any you have dreamed up yourself?
6. What difficulties did he/she have to undergo to achieve his/her goals?
7. In what ways was he/she weak?
8. How did this hurt him/her?
9. How would he/she have made out in our world? Explain.
10. Where did his/her life seem less fulfilled or satisfying?
11. Do most great men/women have large areas of their lives which are not fulfilled?
12. What did friends feel about him/her?

13. How important were their feelings to him/her?
14. In what ways were friends' feelings influential upon him/her?
15. Where did he/she display the greatest courage?
16. Where did he/she display the greatest wisdom?
17. Where did he/she make the greatest contribution?
18. Who benefited from this contribution?
19. Are there any ways he/she lived which would be good for people to follow today?

Sometimes it helps motivate children if they can hear someone they like, respect, or study about give a short summary of his/her own life. Disney Records has a record entitled "Great Moments with Mr. Lincoln," on which Royal Dano speaks as Lincoln and narrates the following part of the autobiography Lincoln was asked to write in 1860 (2):

I was born February 12, 1809 in Hardin County, Kentucky. My mother, who died in my tenth year, was of a family of the name of Hanks. My paternal grandfather, Abraham Lincoln, emigrated from Rockingham County, Virginia, to Kentucky about 1781 or 2, where, a year or two later he was killed by Indians, not in battle but by stealth, when he was laboring to open a farm in the forest.

My father, at the death of his father, was but six years of age; and he grew up literally without education. He removed from Kentucky to what is now Spencer County, Indiana, in my eighth year. It was a wild region, with many bears, and other wild animals still in the woods. There I grew up. We settled in an unbroken forest; and the clearing away of surplus wood was the great task ahead. I was large for my age and had an axe put into my hands at once; and from that to my twenty-third year was almost constantly handling that most useful instrument—less, of course, in plowing and harvesting seasons.

I went to A.B.C. Schools by littles—I think that the aggregate of all my schooling did not amount to one year. What I have in the way of education, I have picked up. I studied English grammar so as to speak and write well, and I nearly mastered the six books of Euclid.

At twenty-one I came to Illinois. At New Salem I studied what I should do—thought of learning the blacksmith trade—thought of trying to study law—rather thought I could not succeed at that without a better education. I borrowed law books, took them home, and went at it in good earnest. In the autumn of 1836 I obtained a law license, removed to Springfield, and commenced practice. In 1846 I was elected to the lower House of Congress. Was not a candidate for re-election. In 1854 the law profession almost superseded the thought of politics in my mind, when the repeal of the Missouri Compromise aroused me as I had never before.

What I have done since then is pretty well known.

If any personal description of me is thought desirable, it may be said I am in height, six feet, four inches, nearly; lean in flesh, weighing, on an average, one hundred and eighty pounds; dark complexion, with coarse black hair, and grey eyes—no other marks or brands recollected.

Yours very truly,
A. *Lincoln*

Display three portrait photographs of Lincoln (Documentary Photo Aids) which were taken in 1860 (without beard), 1863 and 1865 (2). Captions could be placed near the pictures or the questions could be on tape. Some captions might be the following: "How many years elapsed between pictures 1 and 2, 2 and 3, and 1 and 3?" (three years, two years, and five years). "What could have happened during these five years that made him age so much?" (Civil War, problems with Congress, personal problems). Pictures from recent newspapers and magazines are also available that show familiar drastic changes in the president and other public figures.

Questions such as "Do you think it would be possible for an eleven year old girl to get a person elected president of this country?" "What really makes a person vote for one candidate instead of another?" "Have you ever written the president?" "Why do people write to the president?" "What is the proper way to write to the president?" could lead to research on protocol, motives, and results. If the first question were used, a picture (Documentary Photo Aids) showing the letter written in 1860 by eleven year old Grace Bedell of Westfield, New York, to Lincoln and his reply could be mounted near a cassette player which has a recording (by a student) of the girl's letter. It reads (2):

October 15, 1860

Honorable A. Lincoln

Dear Sir:
My father has just come home from the fair and brought home your picture and Mrs. Lincoln's. I am a little girl only eleven years old, but want you should be President of the United States very much so I hope you won't think me very bold to write such a great man as you are. Have you any little girls about as large as I am? If so, give them my love and tell her to write to me if you cannot answer this letter. I have got four brothers and part of them will vote for you anyway and if you will let your whiskers grow I will try and get the rest of them to vote for you. You would look a great deal better for your face is so thin. All the ladies like whiskers and would tease their husbands to vote for you and then

86   Johnson

you would be president. My father is a going to vote for you and if I was a man I would vote for you to, but I will try and get everyone to vote for you that I can. I think that rail fence around your picture makes it look very pretty. I have got a little baby sister. She is nine weeks old and is just as cunning as can be. Will you send your letter direct to Grace Bedell, Westfield, N.Y. I must not write any more. Answer this letter right off. Good bye,

Grace Bedell

One interesting fact about the two letters is that Miss Bedell mailed hers in New York on April 15, 1860 and Lincoln replied on April 19 from Springfield, Illinois, only four days later. This could lead students to write letters to people around the country asking them to reply, stating the date they received the original letters. They might read to discover that mail was faster in 1860 or with the Pony Express that it is today!

Pictures of Presidents Harrison, Lincoln, Garfield, McKinley, Harding, F.D. Roosevelt, and Kennedy might be displayed with the caption, "What, besides being President, do these men have in common?" (They were all elected in multiples of 20 years since 1840 and all died in office.) Or, have students investigate the similarities between people such as Lincoln and Kennedy, as there were many. The December 1965 issue of *Playboy* has an excellent article on this topic (5).

Since *Roots* was published and shown on TV, slavery once again is a topic of much interest. *Jackdaw* kits are packets of primary source information (4). One of these, "The Slave Trade and its Abolition," has such things as old woodcuts of slaves being led to the beach, acclimated, and sold; a copy of an original slave auction advertisement; and the diagram of how slaves were stowed on ship. A very interesting bulletin board could be displayed with captions such as "How was slavery like being a child, housewife, or teacher?"

The filmstrip, "Black Rabbits and White Rabbits" (1), could be shown. In the narration, questions are asked that will lead to further investigation. One copy of an original slave poster (Pioneer Press) shows an auction at the "New Exchange" slave market in New Orleans in 1835. This is the same slave market referred to in *The Slave Dancer*, the 1974 Newbery Award winner. Display the Jackdaw kit, the book, the slave poster, and have a recording of the poster (made by you or a student) to develop motivation for reading more on the topic. Or you might display the auction poster with the want ad section of a local paper and ask students to draw a comparison between buying a slave in 1835 and a car, home, or appliance in 1979. The poster reads as follows (6):

> The owner of the following named and valuable slaves being on the eve of departure of Europe, will cause the same to be offered for sale, at the NEW EXCHANGE, corner of St. Louis and Chartres streets, on Saturday, May 16, at twelve o'clock, viz.
>
> 1. SARAH, a mulatress, aged 45 years, a good cook and accustomed to house work in general, is an excellent and faithful nurse for sick persons, and in every respect a first rate character.
> 2. DENNIS, her son, a mulatto, aged 24 years, a first rate cook and steward for a vessel, having been in that capacity for many years on board one of the Mobil packets; is strictly honest, temperate, and a first rate subject.
> 3. CHOLE, a mulatress, aged 36 years, she is, without exception, one of the most competent servants in the country, a first rate washer and ironer, does up lace, a good cook, and for a bachelor who wishes a housekeeper she would be invaluable; she is also a good ladies' maid, having travelled to the North in that capacity.
> 4. FANNY, her daughter, a mulatress, aged 16 years, speaks French and English, is a superior hairdresser (pupil of Guillliac), a good seamstress and ladies' maid, is smart, intelligent, and a first rate character.
> 5. DANDRIDGE, a mulatto, aged 26 years, a first rate dining room servant, good painter and rough carpenter, and has but few equals for honesty and sobriety.
> 7. NANCY, his wife, aged about 24 years, a confidential house servant, good seamstress, mantuamaker and tailoress, a good cook, washer and ironer, etc.
> 7. MARY ANN, her child, a creole, aged 7 years, speaks French and English, is smart, active and intelligent.
> 8. FANNY or FRANCES, a mulatress, aged 22 years, is a first rate washer and ironer, good cook and house servant, and has an excellent character.
> 9. EMMA, an orphan, aged 10 or 11 years, speaks French and English, has been in the country 7 years, has been accustomed to waiting on tables, serving, etc. is intelligent and active.
> 10. FRANK, a mulatto, aged about 32 years speaks French and English, is a first rate hostler and coachman, understands perfectly well the management of horses, and is, in every respect, a first rate character with the exception that he will occasionally drink, though not an habitual drunkard.
>
> All the above named slaves are acclimated and excellent subjects; they were purchased by their present vendor many years ago, and will, therefore, be severally warranted against all vices and maladies prescribed by law, save and except FRANK, who is fully guaranteed in every other respect but the one above mentioned.

Terms: One-half case, and the other half in notes at six months, drawn and endorsed to the satisfaction of the vendor, with special mortgage on the slaves until final payment. The Acts of Sale to be passed before WILLIAM BOSWELL, Notary Public, at the expense of the purchaser.

New Orleans, May 31, 1835

Following are some suggestions for encouraging students to read and use the library:

1. cartoons
2. questions that relate "heroes" to children
3. pictures (Lincoln et al.)
4. recordings by students (letter to Lincoln)
5. professional records (biography)
6. Jackdaw kits (slavery)
7. primary source information (auction)
8. newspapers (ads)
9. filmstrips (Black Rabbits)
10. award winning books (*Slave Dancer*)

We have to do something to prevent our students from moving away from books. We do not want them to end up like Lucy in a "Peanuts" comic strip some years ago. The three frames showed her sitting at her desk in school and saying:

1. Maam?
2. I'm not sure about this first question.
3. As a matter of fact, I don't think I can answer any of these questions.
4. Maybe I could just help the custodian sweep the halls.

References

1. *Black Rabbits and White Rabbits*. Pleasantview, New York: Warren Schloat Productions.
2. Documentary Photo Aids, Box 956, Mount Dora, Florida 32757.
3. "Great Moments with Mr. Lincoln," Buena Vista Records, Walt Disney Productions, 1964.
4. Jackdaw Kits, edited by John Langdon-Darles, Jackdaw Publications, London. Available through Social Studies School Service, 19000 Culner Boulevard, Culner City, California 90239.
5. "Lincoln and Kennedy," *Playboy*, December 1965, 110-114.
6. Pioneer Press, Harriman, Tennessee, formerly produced primary source material but is no longer in business.
7. Sasnowski, Frank W. "Report Making the Cartoon Way," *Teacher*, March 1975, 75-77.

Magic Moments with Media

Jeanne Eisenbarth, LeAnn Green, and Margaret Sloan
Rochester, Minnesota, Public Schools

Paperbacks: Extending Out and Beyond*

The object in this project was to extend reading beyond basals into various kinds of media. Two paperback book titles were selected to fit the theme of each unit of the basal readers in grades four through six (thirty-six titles in all). Fifteen copies of each title were purchased and packaged for classroom use. For each title, an activity sheet was developed to provide the extension out and beyond. A conscious effort was made to provide creative projects—projects which would enhance the appreciation for the paperback under study and would provide a balance of activities among the various language arts and other curriculum areas.

The project was limited to top readers because the reading levels of the paperbacks varied and it was impossible to accomplish our objective if only books with controlled vocabularies were used. Many of the books were considerably more difficult than the grade level placement of the students reading them, but the top readers did rise to the challenge.

Purpose of Project

The goal was to challenge the top readers in grades four through six to extend their skills and interests beyond the

---

*Developed by Jeanne Eisenbarth and the Elementary Reading Teachers, Independent School District 535, Rochester, Minnesota.

basal; to develop further their discussion techniques, their organizational and library and research skills, and their ability to work independently and in small groups with group leaders; to extend their appreciation for good literature; and to promote the reading habit as a lifetime pursuit.

Contents

Following are copies of nine of the thirty-six activity sheets developed for the project:

The project was most effective in getting students meaningfully involved with good books and with projects extending out of the books and the basal reader themes. The only problem was that the other students wanted paperback books for their classes as well.

HELEN KELLER - 4

1. Construct a time line showing the progress of events in Helen's life.
2. Divide your group into pairs or partners. Have one child be Helen and the other be Annie Sullivan. Direct Helen to close her eyes while Annie writes words in her hand. Try simple one-syllable words at first (dog, love, jump). Later, try sentences. After awhile have the partners switch roles.
3. What was the most important thing Annie showed Helen? Why is communication between people important? Construct a mural showing the different ways people can communicate.
4. Name some ways you communicate with your friends. How

would you communicate if you lost one or more of these ways?

5. Request the librarian to locate a book in Braille. Have the students discuss the Braille alphabet and how the dots are made.

6. Invite a blind person to come and speak to the class. Ask the person to demonstrate how to read and write Braille.

7. Invite a person from the school system or department of the handicapped to come to your class and speak. Also request to see a Braille typewriter if one is available.

ISLAND OF THE BLUE DOLPHINS - 4

1. Construct a two or three dimensional map of the Island of the Blue Dolphins. Include the places where Karana lived; the cave where the dogs lived; and the beach, cliffs, and coral caves.

2. On a globe, try to plot the location of the island using the information stated or inferred in the book. Be able to defend your choice.

3. Draw a picture of Karana's home on the island using descriptions from the book beginning with Chapter 12.

4. Using small rocks, stones, and bits of wood, construct weapons and tools Karana might have used for protection and for hunting.

5. Pretend your ship sank at sea and you were washed up on the beach of a small island. Write a diary, complete with diagrams, on the steps you would take for survival. The island is inhabited only by wild animals.

6. Research and sketch the kinds of birds mentioned in the book. Where are these birds generally found? Does their general location help pinpoint where the island is?

7. Many native names have special meanings. Research to find out what your first and middle name means and what nationality it might be.

8. Make a list of the superstitions mentioned in the book. Compare them to our culture today. What superstitions do we have?

9. Make necklaces or headbands from shells or other materials Karana might have found on the beach of the island.

10. Draw or paint an underwater scene of the animals or fish mentioned in the story.

1. The early Polynesians believed in many gods as part of their religion and ritual. List the different gods mentioned in the story.

>Moana—the Sea God
>Maui—the God of the Fisherman
>Mata Iki—the God of the Eaters-of-Men

2. Make a dictionary of Polynesian language used in the story with comparable English words.

purau	maral
tupapau	mape
Aia	tamanu
Aue	motu tabu
himene	fei
pahua	artu
pala	pukatea
Te mori	puaa viri
poi	puaa
pareu	feke
Ai	

3. Organize a food tasting party with several of the foods mentioned in the book. Example: bananas—steamed or cooked in some way. Write a recipe for one food that was mentioned.
4. Construct a model canoe, raft, or war canoe.
5. The book does not say whether Mafatu lived or died as he reached his home island. Write an extended ending to the book either with the boy as a live hero or as a dead hero as he arrived in the canoe.
6. Using scraps of material, cut and tie dye an example of a loincloth that the boy might have worn.
7. Make a relief map of the island as accurately as you can from the book.
8. Macrame a small fish net somewhat like the one Mafatu made.

1. Research and discuss the early African slave trade in America. Ask you librarian for help.
2. Make a time line or mural depicting the events in Amos' life.

1725	1740	1769	1773
Amos sold as a black slave at age 15 to Caleb Copeland	Amos resold to Ichabod Richardson at age 30	Amos becomes free man at age 59	Amos frees and marries Lily at age 63

1778	1770	1781
Amos frees and marries Lydia at age 68	Amos frees and marries Violet at age 69	Amos, Violet, Clyndia move to Jaffrey, N.H.

3. Research and discuss the money system presented in the book. Find out the equivalent in American money for British pounds and shillings.
4. Make a map and locate the different towns in which Amos lived. Stick on the map small slips of paper indicating the events that took place in each town.
5. Amos learned the tanning profession as a slave. On page 109 there is a picture of the various tanning tools Amos used. Make a list of each tool pictured and tell how it is used. What other things did Amos use?
6. Research and discuss several black spirituals, especially those mentioned in the book. Example: "Jordan River" and "Swing Low, Sweet Chariot." Have the children listen to them and sing them. Ask your music teacher for help.
7. Write to the Chamber of Commerce of East Jaffrey, New Hampshire, and request information on Amos Fortune and his burial site. Also, check the acknowledgement section of the book for other names and addresses.
8. Invite a speaker to come to your class and explain the tanning process. How is it done today? Compare and contrast the tanning process today with that of Amos' day.
9. Read another book about Amos Fortune listing some of the important facts about his life found in both books. If the

facts in one book do not agree with those in the other book, consult a third book. Discuss what you found with a teammate.

CADDIE WOODLAWN - 5

1. Research the massacre in New Ulm. What happened to cause it? How did it end?
2. Request the music teacher to locate some of the songs mentioned in the book.
3. Imagine that you are Caddie. Plan how you would spend $1. Locate information on how much things cost in the 1860s-1870s.
4. Construct a miniature birch bark canoe.
5. Change the ending of the story so that the Woodlawns vote to go to England. Tell how you think their lives would have been different.
6. Pretend you are Caddie. Write an article for your school paper or a letter to a friend telling about a week in school.
7. Read another story about a pioneer girl and her life. Compare the problems of Caddie's family with those of Laura Ingalls Wilder's family. Use *On the Banks of Plum Creek* and *By the Shores of Silver Lake* for references.
8. Write a character description of Caddie. What is she like? What are her favorite things to do?

DAY OF GLORY - 5

1. Construct on cards a time line of events as they unfold hour by hour. Example: On each card put the *day, time, setting* and *characters* involved.

April 19, 1775	April 19, 1775
7:00 p.m.	8:00 p.m.
On the road to Lexington from Boston	Dr. Warren's house—Boston
Solomon Brown returns to Lexington carrying a message for Adams and Hancock	A meeting of the committee

2. Pretend that your are a newscaster, such as Edward R. Murrow, and, with the events from the book, give an hour by hour "You Were There" TV newscast.

3. Compile a list of terms relevant to the time period in the book. Also list comparable English words. Example:

cooper	barrel maker	cordwainer
grenadiers	bumpkins	on the green
huzza	Minute Men	Tories

4. Construct a map of Boston and the surrounding towns. Include the following towns:

Lexington	Concord	Roxbury
North Bridge	Dorchester	Brookline
Menotomy	Salem	Bunker Hill
Acton	Cambridge	Charles River
Charlestown	Danvers	Gloucester

Perhaps the map could be an electric map using small colored lights to show the path of the action.

5. Make a list of the main characters, indicating which side each was on.

American	British
Sam Adams	General Gage
John Hancock	Major Mitchell
Paul Revere	Colonel Smith
Joseph Warren	Major Pitcairn
Solomon Brown	John Howe
	Captain Pole
	Captain Laurie
	Lord Percy

Choose a few favorite characters and write several clues describing each character. Read the clues until someone can guess the character.

6. Research fife and drum music used during the Revolutionary War. Locate the following songs and have the children learn them. Ask your music teacher for help.

"White Cockade"
"Chevy Chase"
"Yankee Doodle"
"British Grenadier"

7. Research different artillery muskets, musket balls, and bayonets.

PAGE BOY OF CAMELOT - 6

1. Research falconry. What is it? How are the birds trained? Of what value is falconry? Compare this description of

Eisenbarth, Green, and Sloan

falconry to that in *Adam of the Road* and *My Side of the Mountain*.

2. Pretend you are a knight or a knight's lady. Design a coat of arms for your family name.
3. Research the Knights of the Round Table. How did it begin? Who started it? How did it work?
4. Make a list of old English terms from the book. List their modern American counterparts in the opposite column.
5. Request the music teacher for a copy of the record "Camelot." Discuss the people and places mentioned in the songs. How well do the songs relate to actual history of the era of King Arthur?
6. Research *excalibar*. What is it? How was it used? Make colored drawings and label the parts.
7. Research the progression of a boy to knighthood.
8. Make a model of a medieval castle showing the interior layout.
9. Compare what home life would be like then and now. What decisions would you make? Would you choose to leave home and become an "apprentice" at a castle?

ADAM OF THE ROAD - 6

1. Research falconry. What is it? How are the birds trained? Of what value is falconry? What are the differences among lanners-lannerets, gerfalcons, merlins, and goshawks?
2. Make a collection of the plural forms used in the story (e.g., flight of swallows, walk of snipe, gaggle of geese, blush of boys, bevy of girls). Extend the collection to include plural forms used today.
3. Make a collection of unfamiliar words classifying them under broad categories:

Places	Things	Animals and Birds
almonry	wallet	jennet
heath	quintain	lanner and lanneret
tiltyard	vestcoats	gerfalcon
solar	surcoats	merlin
pastern	ewers	goshawk
buttery	hauberk	
mews	jesses	
	hoods	
	coif	
	distaff	

Food	Music	People
pottage	viol	almoner
leeks	harp	harper
kidney pie	lay of _____	bailiff
comfits	psalteries	falconer
	tabors	yeoman
	portmanteau	leige lady
		carving squire
		saracen
		palmer

4. Make a collection of figurative language used at the time of Adam. Try to think of comparable language used today (sweet as honey, sharp as a tack, whey faced, silk looking, past his meddlesome youth, not a kid anymore).

5. Draw a diagram and write directions for the game, Tilting at the Quintain. Contact the physical education department for a similar game.

6. Write a report about minstrelsy. What was it? Why was it popular? Why was it important? Compare minstrelsy with methods of communication today. Contrast minstrelsy and TV as to purpose, cost, impact.

7. Contact the music department. Listen to minstrel songs. Compose a minstrel song. Using a puppet created by a student, share the song with the class.

8. Research food preservation at the time of Adam. Compare with methods used today. Class demonstration.

9. Compare and contrast inn/hotel prices and accommodations offered at an inn during the time of Adam and a well known local hotel or motel.

10. Construct a castle locating the various rooms and areas mentioned in *Adam of the Road.*

11. Draw a map of the area Adam traveled in search of Nick. Adam's travels could be shown with one color, Roger's with another color, and Jankin's with a third color.

12. Research and compare the governmental organization at the time of Adam with England today. A time line could be constructed to show the change from a king to a prime minister at the head.

13. Sample pottage and wastell bread. What were they? How were they made? Try to locate recipes for them.

14. Do a skit of "The Fall of Adam," fashioning it after the skit described in the story.

Eisenbarth, Green, and Sloan

1. Draw a picture or construct a model of the interior layout of Sam's treehouse, using the description in the book.
2. Make a chart of the different plants and roots used in the book. Include how the food was prepared, what it tasted like, and its use. Example:

Food	How to Prepare	Tastes Like	Use
1. Acorn pancakes			
2. Cattail roots			
3. Arrow leaf			
4. Dandelions			
5. Jack-in-the pulpit roots			
6. Wild garlic			
7. Hickory sticks			

3. Research different types of edible plants and look for different recipes using these plants and roots. Check with your librarian for books written about natural foods. Euell Gibbons' *Stalking the Good Life* is an adult book that you often hear mentioned. You could get this at the public library.
4. Invite an ecologist to come to your classroom and speak on different types of edible plants and roots.
5. Make up your *own* recipes using various edible plants and roots.
6. Construct a wooden fish hook as sketched and described in the book.
7. Research and build model game snares and traps as sketched and described in the book.
8. Make a large cube and decorate each side with scenes from the story.
9. Construct a slide willow whistle as sketched and described in the book.
10. You are lost in an isolated area. How will you survive? Describe the type of area you selected. List what things you

would do first, second, etc. From your notes, plan a two minute speech telling about your "experience."

11. Research and construct different types of feeding stations for animals. Use *Open Highways 4* as a reference, if it is available, or ask your librarian.

12. Discuss with a partner what it would be like to be isolated from other people for several months. Tell or write what you could do to keep from getting lonely, bored, or frightened.

Biographical Sketches with Videotape

Objectives

1. To provide an introduction to a biography unit.
2. To provide instruction and an example for students to follow in the reading of biographies.
3. To show students a different way to report on a biography.

Procedures

The students were introduced to a biography unit by a teacher presentation of an example of how students would "report" on the biographies after they had read them. A different way of reporting on their biography was explained and then shown to the students by the teachers. Each teacher assumed a character in a biography and, with appropriate costumes, pretended to be that character. A talk show format was used as one teacher interviewed three other teachers.

The following examples were given as aids for the students in preparing their questions for their interviews and for a better understanding of the objectives of the biography project.

A videotape of the teachers' example was made for future performances for junior high classes.

Extension

The students chose their biographies and then partners for interviews. They wrote questions for their characters and

Eisenbarth, Green, and Sloan

appeared with costumes and necessary props for their interviews. Students became interested in other biographies when they heard the interviews.

Biography Interviews

Students *A* and *B* will work in pairs in reporting their biographies. *A* will play the role of the person whose biography he has read. He will use costuming or stage properties to better portray his biography. *B* will be the interviewer and ask questions (prepared by both *A* and *B*) of *A* who is portraying the subject of his biography.

The team will then reverse the procedure with *A* becoming the interviewer and questioning *B* about the subject of *B*'s biography.

Although you will design your questions to fit the subject of your biography, some questions (typical of an explorer, for example) might be:

1. Were there influences in your early life that had any effect on your decision to become an explorer?
2. When did you decide to become an explorer?
3. How much training did your work require?
4. How much did others (friends, family, teachers) influence you in choosing your life work?
5. To whom do you give credit for most of your success?
6. Do you have any other interests?
7. Did you experience any failures in life?
8. What do you feel is your greatest achievement in life?
9. Does your achievement benefit all mankind?
10. How do you feel you may have affected other people in your life?
11. What difficulties did you have to overcome in accomplishing your purposes?

Biography

A biography is usually a series of events that happens to the main character. A point of view is the way in which an author or others in the life of the character see him. Fill in the following diagrams after inserting your subject's name in the blank.

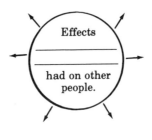

Effects
_____
had on other
people.

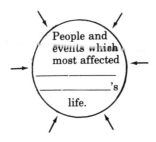

People and
events which
most affected
_____
_____'s
life.

Additional Ways to Involve Students with Literature through the Use of Videotapes

1. Writing a play and taping it for other classes to enjoy.
2. Writing book reviews and taping them for other classes.
3. Writing stories for self-evaluation and taping them for others to enjoy or use for self-evaluation.
4. Dressing pupils as characters from books and advertising that books are exciting to read.
5. Making books for the library and explaining to others how this could be done. (Students love to be authors.)
6. Taping poems and illustrating them to show how exciting poetry can be.
7. Taping proper use of library materials (Reader's Guide, Atlas, encyclopedias). This tape could be used on an individual basis or for an entire class.
8. Taping procedures for using library materials and orientation for elementary students before they visit the junior high library.
9. Syllabication in third grade.

10. Synonyms and antonyms (advanced children could prepare these).

A Selected Bibliography of Biographies
Junior High

Boylston, Helen Dore. *Clara Barton, Founder of American Red Cross.* New York: Random House, 1955.

Bryan, J. *The World's Greatest Showman: The Life of P.T. Barnum.* New York: Random House, 1956.

Brown, John Mason. *Daniel Boone: The Opening of the Wilderness.* New York: Random House, 1952.

Clapp, Patricia. *Dr. Elizabeth: The Story of the First Woman Doctor.* New York: Lothrop, Lee, and Shepard, 1974.

Devaney, John. *The Bobby Orr Story.* New York: Random House, 1973.

Dugan, James. *Undersea Explorer: Story of Captain Costeau.* New York: Harper and Row, 1957.

Garst, Shannon. *Buffalo Bill.* New York: Julian Messner, 1969.

Garst, Shannon. *Jim Bridger: Greatest of the Mountain Men.* Boston: Houghton Mifflin, 1952.

Garst, Shannon. *Kit Carson: Trail Blazer and Scout.* New York: Julian Messner, 1967.

Graham, Frank. *Lou Gehrig.* New York: G.P. Putnam's Sons, 1942.

Grey, Elizabeth. *Friend within the Gates: The Story of Nurse Edith Cavell.* Boston: Houghton Mifflin, 1961.

Gunther, John. *Julius Caesar.* New York: Random House, 1959.

Holbrook, Stewart H. *Davy Crockett from the Backwoods of Tennessee to the Alamo.* New York: Random House, 1955.

Ketchum, Richard M. *Will Rogers: The Man and His Times.* New York: American Heritage Publishing, 1973.

Mellor, William Bancroft. *General Patton: The Last Cavalier.* New York: G.P. Putnam's Sons, 1971.

Monsell, Helen Albee. *Dolly Madison: Quaker Girl.* Indianapolis: Bobbs-Merrill, 1961.

Ross, Nancy Wilson. *Joan of Arc.* New York: Random House, 1953.

Schoor, Gener. *The Jim Thorpe Story.* New York: Julian Messner, 1951.

Shippen, Katherine B. *Leif Eriksson: First Voyager to America.* New York: Harper and Row, 1951.

Silverman, Al. *Mickey Mantle: Mister Yankee.* New York: G.P. Putnam's Sons, 1963.

Steinberg, Alfred. *Harry S. Truman.* New York: G.P. Putnam's Sons, 1963.

Stevenson, Augusta. *Abe Lincoln: Frontier Boy.* Indianapolis: Bobbs-Merrill, 1959.

Sullivan, George. *Wilt Chamberlain*. New York: Grosset and Dunlap, 1970.

Valens, E.G. *A Long Way Up: The Story of Jill Kenmont*. New York: Harper and Row, 1966.

Weil, Ann. *Betsy Ross: Girl of Old Philadelphia*. Indianapolis: Bobbs-Merrill, 1961.

Weil, Ann. *John Quincy Adams: Boy Patriot*. Indianapolis: Bobbs-Merrill, 1963.

White, Anne Terry. *George Washington Carver*. New York: Random House, 1953.

White, Stewart Edward. *Daniel Boone, Wilderness Scout*. Garden City, New York: Doubleday, 1922.

Winders, Gertrude. *Jim Bowie: Boy with a Hunting Knife*. Indianapolis: Bobbs-Merrill, 1961.

Wise, Winifred E. *Jane Addams of Hull House*. New York: Harcourt, Brace Jovanovich, 1963.